MY CREED:
TO DO THE BEST I CAN,
DESPITE THE ODDS

LESSONS FROM LIFE'S UNCERTAINTIES

TRUE STRENGTH COMES FROM EMBRACING LIFE'S CHAOS WITH COURAGE, CLARITY, CONVICTION, AND COMPASSION

BY ROHIT BASSI

ROHIT BASSI

COPYRIGHT ©2025 BY ROHIT BASSI

ALL RIGHTS RESERVED

DEDICATION

To the ones who are doing great. To the ones giving their best, even when the world fails to notice. To the ones who pour their hearts into every moment, only to feel stuck, unseen, or unheard. To the ones who have stopped caring about applause but never stop showing up. To the ones who want to give up. To the ones who have given up.

This book is for you.

It is for the dreamers who wrestle with doubts and fears yet dare to keep dreaming. For those who battle against cultural expectations, peer pressure, and the heavy weight of their own inner voice—only to rise again, scarred but stronger.

It is also for the lazy ones, the ones who procrastinate endlessly, paralysed by overthinking or crushed by their own inertia. For those who let life slip by because the weight of getting it right as per society standards feels unbearable.

MY CREED: TO DO THE BEST I CAN, DESPITE THE ODDS

It is for the silent fighters, the weary warriors, and the ones who get up every single day despite the ache in their souls. It is for those who carry the invisible battles that no one else can see, and for those who find courage in the chaos.

It is for the humble souls who work tirelessly in the shadows, and for the arrogant dreamers who unapologetically claim their place in the sun. It is for the bold, the timid, the proud, and the self-doubting.

It is for everyone—the whole mixture of humanity trying, failing, and sometimes thriving in this universe of infinite possibilities.

May this book be a reminder that your efforts, seen or unseen, matter. May it be a small spark for the light you already carry within. And may it find you, not when you want to disappear, but when you are ready to be found.

This book is dedicated to you. To all of you. Always.

ACKNOWLEDGMENT

Like life, this book has been a journey through the pain and joy of existence itself—shaped by moments of stillness, chaos, and everything in between.

To my family and loved ones, thank you for being my sanctuary, my safe space, my encouragement, and my grounding. Your presence has been a massive strength in the judgmental, ego-driven world we live in.

To those who tried to push me, force me, or fit me into their mould—I resisted, ignored, and stood firm in my younger years. Yes, it made me bitter. Yes, I lost my peace. But as time passed, I learned to walk away—not out of weakness, but because I no longer needed to fight battles that did not serve me.

To those who judged me, misunderstood me, or chose to leave—thank you for being part of the story. You taught me how to move forward, first with resistance and frustration, and later, with the quiet strength of politely walking away.

To my loved ones, friends, colleagues, and clients—your stories, questions, and challenges gave me a multifaceted mirror to see life from countless perspectives, like the multiverse itself. You reminded me that courage, clarity, conviction, compassion and laughter go a long way.

And to you, the reader—thank you for joining me in this space. For walking through these pages as I share reflections, illusions, and the humour life throws at us. My aspiration is simple: may you find a piece of yourself here and carry it forward with grace and grit.

This book was crafted with care, integrity, and respect for originality. The creation process involved reflecting and journaling to capture key ideas and themes, drafting chapters based on personal experiences and insights, and using AI assistance to refine drafts, deepen narratives, and enhance structure while preserving authenticity. Each chapter was meticulously revised to align with the book's message and emotional depth, followed by multiple reviews to ensure originality, coherence, and personal expression.

AI played a supportive role, enhancing creativity and structure without replacing original thought or human expression. Every word and idea originate from my experiences, readings and reflections, intended to inspire and encourage readers authentically.

This process adhered to ethical standards and creativity. The work remains deeply personal and original, shaped by my journey and the wisdom gained along the way.

Thank you for being part of this journey. May the stories and reflections within these pages bring you growth and clarity as they did for me.

With respect, love, and gratitude,
Rohit Bassi

FOREWORD

I've had the privilege of knowing Rohit Bassi for only a few years but somehow, we share a deep connection despite the time spent together. We caught up again recently and shared our journey filled with stories, laughter, and an unshakable belief in living life with purpose and resilience.

Rohit is not just a friend — he is a fellow traveller on the road of pursuing dreams, facing challenges head-on, and finding joy even in the darkest moments. His life, like mine, has been a testament to the power of embracing setbacks with a smile and turning obstacles into stepping stones.

When Rohit first spoke to me about *"My Creed: To Do The Best I Can, Despite The Odds",* I instantly resonated with its message. Thanks, Rohit, for trusting me to write your foreword! Life, as we both know, doesn't hand out success on a silver platter. Instead, it tests us, pushes us beyond our limits, and often knocks us down. But it's what we choose to do in those moments that defines us. Rohit's creed — a personal declaration to be the best version of oneself no matter the circumstances — is a philosophy we both live by. It's about daring to dream, staying true to your values, and finding strength even when the odds seem insurmountable.

Throughout this book, Rohit shares wisdom born from real experiences, blending the practical with the profound, the painful with the inspirational. His words will challenge you to reflect on your own journey and, more importantly, to commit to your own creed of living with courage, authenticity, and relentless positivity.

Our friendship has taught me that true resilience isn't just about perseverance. It's about choosing to smile through adversity — not as a mask, but as a mark of defiance and hope. We've both faced our share of trials, and through it all, we've cheered each other on, reminding ourselves that the road may be long, but the rewards are worth every stumble and every step. As you turn the pages of this powerful book, you'll discover that Rohit isn't just telling his story. He's inviting you to craft your own. Let his words be a guide, a spark of motivation, and a reminder that you, too, can rise above any challenge with grace, determination, and a heart full of purpose.

It is my deepest honour to be a part of Rohit's journey. I hope it will inspire you as much as it has inspired me to never stop striving, never stop smiling, and always pursue your best, no matter what life throws your way.

FREDA LIU
https://fredaliu.com/

Freda Liu is a renowned global speaker, author of seven impactful books, and an award-winning broadcast journalist. Having conducted over 10,000 interviews with some of the world's most influential thinkers, she is a trusted voice in media and business. A passionate advocate for sustainability and social enterprises, Freda supports causes like clean water initiatives and women's empowerment. Her work inspires transformation, blending resilience, wisdom, and a commitment to making a difference.

IMPORTANT NOTE MUST READ

Before you continue through these pages, I always do my best to speak with honesty and compassion. Life has infinite possibilities. The stories, reflections, and insights shared in this book are drawn from my personal experiences and the lessons I have gathered from others. I am only sharing what I have come across, experienced, seen, or heard of.

If you are facing chronic issues such as financial hardship, poverty, health issues, depression, anxiety, trauma, abuse, suicidal tendency or any other profound emotional, mental, physical or spiritual pain, please know this: You deserve compassionate, professional support. Seeking help from qualified professionals—whether therapists, counsellors, financial advisors, medical experts, or support groups—is an act of courage, never weakness. This book is not a substitute for professional guidance.

The reflections within these pages may inspire or resonate with you. They may also challenge you or feel difficult to connect with at times. That is okay.

Personal truths are rarely universal. My words are shared not as absolute answers but as an invitation for you to explore your own truth, your own healing, and your own wisdom. You may agree with some insights here. You may strongly disagree with others. That, too, is welcome. Growth is never about blind acceptance; it is about questioning, reflecting, and finding what aligns with your path.

Above all, be gentle with yourself. Healing is not linear. Transformation is not a race. And you are never alone in your journey. If anything within these pages encourages you to seek deeper support, please honour that call with the same compassion you would offer a loved one. May this book serve as a mirror, not a map—reflecting possibilities, not dictating paths. Thank you for being here, for reading, and for choosing to explore the depths of your own experience.

With respect and compassion,
Rohit Bassi

WELCOME TO THE CHAOS: Life, Love, and Illusions

Dear Reader,

Life, in all its messiness and beauty, is nothing short of chaos—and yet, perfectly fine when we achieve that zen mode, even if it is just for a split second. Yes, it is a cliché, a paradox, and a labyrinth wrapped in layers I continue to navigate.

It pulls you. It pushes you. Some say it tests you. Others insist it teaches you. And sometimes—when you least expect it—it makes you laugh. For some, it happens a lot. For others, very little. And for a few, they are simply miserable. I will admit, I am still learning to embrace this chaos—not always as a burden (though, let us be honest, many times I do), but as the raw material for living fully. And yes, I still fail miserably at it, even today.

We are sold so many stories about life. Many preach that success—measured by money—is everything.

Others promise that love will solve all problems. Then there are those who declare, *"everything happens for a reason."*

Yet buried beneath these illusions is the unspoken truth: Life owes you nothing.

Dreams come with no guarantees and can turn into nightmares. People will disappoint you, and here is the kicker—you will disappoint yourself, too. And yet, here we are breathing, stumbling, laughing, and somehow, finding our way.

This book is not a guide. It will not give you answers or offer neatly packaged solutions wrapped with shiny bows. I am not here to preach, push, or save you from the mess. I am here to invite you—gently, compassionately, and with raw honesty—to reflect, question, and perhaps laugh out loud along the way.

The book is not here to give you a three, five, eight or whatever step plan or sugarcoat the realities of life. Instead, it invites you to dive into the chaos with open eyes and an open heart. Through raw stories,

reflective insights, and lessons learned the hard way, we will explore what it truly means to navigate life's beautiful mess.

As you go through these pages, you will notice some ideas coming up more than once—concepts like uncertainty, imperfection, and resilience. This is because these events take on different meanings in different parts of life, whether it is personal growth, relationships, or work. Life has a way of showing the same message in many forms, and this book reflects that. Each chapter tells its own story, but together, they create a fuller picture, inviting you to reflect, question, and see your own experiences in a different way.

Life never flows as we want it to. It stumbles. It jerks you forward, pulls you back, and throws chaos at you when you least expect it. This book is not here to give you neat, tidy solutions or offer you a smooth ride—it is as abrupt and messy as life itself. The chapters will reflect that. Some are raw and intimate; others are reflective and analytical. They will not flow seamlessly, because neither does life. What you will find here are tools—practical, infinite, and adaptable—that will not necessarily promise to fix matters but will help you stand firm in the storms of life. This is not a manual for perfection. It is a guide for navigating the chaos with great strength.

The lessons within these pages come from my life story—a life of battles fought, peace sought, relationships tested, patterns repeated (yes, they still are), and oh my, the unnecessary drama. Some experiences brought joy, others carried pain, and then there were those that were both painful and expensive. Yet, each one communicated me something worth sharing—the bold and beautiful, the good, the bad, and the ugly.

So, welcome. Welcome to the chaos of life, love, and illusions. Thank you for choosing to walk through these pages with me. Each chapter is raw, honest, and perhaps familiar to you in ways only you will know.

Together, let us explore the beauty of the unknown and the humour in the contradictions we carry. May you find the courage to face your truths, the clarity to cut through the noise, the conviction to keep going, and the compassion to embrace yourself fully. Above all, may you discover the determination to do your best—despite the odds because that is your creed.

With trust and determination,

Rohit Bassi

www.rohitbassi.com

PART I: The Illusions We Live By

Life is full of stories—some we tell ourselves, some we are told, and many others we unknowingly inherit. Stories that shape the way we think, behave, and perceive the world around us. These stories create illusions—false realities that feel so real, we cling to them for dear life.

We are told that certainty exists. We are sold the belief that dreams with goals and actions alone are enough to change everything. We are encouraged to get out of the so-called *"comfort zone,"* as if discomfort automatically leads to growth. We are preached a formula: *"You are the average of the five people around you."* Who makes these rules? And why do we buy into them so easily?

Here's the truth: Life owes us nothing, and yet we have sold ourselves illusions that it does. We live in a world where guarantees are expected, picture perfect outcomes are romanticised, and success is defined by yardsticks handed down to us by someone else. And when these illusions shatter—as they inevitably

do—what happens to us? We lose ourselves. We feel betrayed, bitter, and confused. "Why me?" we ask, as if life broke some imaginary contract.

But life owes no explanations.

I invite you to pause and look at these illusions with clarity. This is not about blame or judgement. It is not about pointing fingers at society, teachers, parents, or ourselves. It is about uncovering the false promises we have been fed and freeing ourselves from their grip.

Certainty? An illusion.
Dreams with goals and actions? Simply delusional.
Cutting out toxic people? We all carry toxicity towards someone, especially ourselves.

And yet, here's where it gets beautiful: When you let go of these illusions, you make room for something greater. You begin to see life as it truly is—messy, uncertain, and breathtakingly real.

There is freedom in knowing that nothing is guaranteed. There is strength in facing reality as it is—not as we wish it to be. And there is peace in releasing ourselves from the lies we hold onto so tightly.

In the chapters to come, I will share reflections, questions, and stories—raw, honest, and often humorous—that will encourage you to challenge these illusions. This is not an invitation to cynicism. It is an invitation to courage—the courage to unlearn, question, and rewrite your relationship with life.

Welcome to Part I: The Illusions We Live By. Let us begin.

Chapter 1: The Illusion of Certainty

When was the last time you felt absolutely, undeniably certain—so convinced that nothing could shake your belief? Certain that life was steady, predictable, and under control?

Maybe it was a job that felt secure. A relationship you believed would last forever. A plan so neatly drawn up that—sure, maybe failure or doubt did cross your mind—but you pushed it aside because certainty felt so...certain.

Certainty can feel powerful. It can feel comfortable, like a warm blanket that quietly suffocates while promising safety. More often than not, what we think of as comfort is actually laziness or complacency wearing a disguise.

It is stagnation. Stagnation, like water that refuses to flow, starts to reek of foul smell like a cesspit. You know what I'm talking about—the kind of certainty that stops you from questioning, exploring, or moving in flow.

It's the voice that says, "This is good enough. Why bother?" You stop showing up for yourself. You stop moving forward. You settle—not because you're happy but because you're scared of what lies beyond the familiar.

The job? You cling to it because it's "safe," not because it fulfils you. The relationship? You stay because it's predictable, not because it's alive. The plan? You follow it because it feels easy, not because it excites you. And then, just when you think you've nailed it—life shakes you awake.

Certainty feels safe. But what we think is safety is often a slow, silent decay. The moment you stop questioning, stop exploring, stop moving—you are not safe. You are stuck. And when you are stuck long enough, life will come in swinging to shake you loose. The job disappears. The relationship crumbles. The plan falls apart. And you? You are left standing in the ruins, wondering how you never saw it coming.

No, my friend. You were stuck. You simply did not see it yet. You see, certainty is a temporary illusion. It's nice when it's here, but it's also deceptive. It lulls you into thinking you're in control when you're really avoiding growth.

The 2020 COVID chaos ripped the illusion apart in real-time. Entire careers vanished overnight. Some people woke up secure and went to bed jobless. Businesses folded, bank accounts drained, and suddenly, the so-called 'stable' life was gone. If certainty was real, it would have saved them. But certainty is a myth we tell ourselves to feel in control."

The teachings on impermanence from the east remind us that nothing in life is fixed, and peace comes from accepting this reality.

Everything in life flows—your job, your relationships, your health, your plans. Life is like a river; it moves whether you're ready or not. And when you cling to certainty, you're demanding to freeze that river.

What happens then? The water goes stagnant. And stagnant water reeks—of missed opportunities, of what-ifs, of quiet regrets that whisper at night.

Certainty can be comforting, but it's also limiting. It is the enemy of growth when you hold onto it too tightly.

∞

EXPLORATION TIME
So, what if certainty has been holding you back? What then?

Acknowledge where you have clung to certainty out of fear rather than fulfilment. The harm caused by stagnation is not a reflection of your worth—recognize it without absorbing it.

Set shields. You can value stability while still challenging yourself to grow. Draw clear lines where necessary to stop becoming stagnant.

Seek support. Lean on friends, mentors, or your community—growth becomes easier when you share your experiences with those who uplift you.

Turn discomfort into exploration. Use the moments where certainty crumbled to fuel self-discovery, personal growth, and the courage to take small calculative risks.

So, what do we do? We face uncertainty with equanimity. Equanimity is not giving up. It is not indifference. It's standing steady when life pulls the rug out from under you. It's enjoying certainty when it's here—really being present in it—while knowing it will pass. Equanimity allows you to say, 'I may not know what happens next, but I trust myself enough to figure it out.'

Most people crumble when certainty collapses. They panic, cling, beg for things to go back to 'normal.' But equanimity? Equanimity is standing still while the storm howls around you. Not because you are unshaken, but because you know that fear will not save you. You let the storm do its thing, knowing you will still be standing when it passes. That is power. That is presence.

And if you waver? If fear grips your chest and your knees buckle? That is human. Equanimity is not about being some unbreakable force—it is about choosing to breathe through the chaos, to ground yourself when the world spins wild. It is knowing that you can bend, shake, even fall, and still rise.

Equanimity is like standing in the stillness of the eye of the storm. It is not the absence of chaos, nor is it a state of complete peace. Instead, it is the profound strength of recognising pain and suffering, accepting them without resistance or denial, and choosing to move through them with kindness and care.

It is not about erasing discomfort or pretending challenges vanish. Equanimity allows you to acknowledge life's turbulence while remaining steady. It is the ability to sit with the pain, understanding its presence, and navigate through it with compassion—both for yourself and for others.

In this way, equanimity becomes an anchor. It shields you from being overwhelmed by life's storms and offers the grace to pass through them, transforming struggle into resilience and suffering into understanding. It is the art of being present in the moment, no matter how chaotic, with a heart that remains open and a mind that remains steady.

Stagnant water stinks, but flowing rivers bring life. Enjoy certainty when it's here, and trust

yourself to be in flow, even when the next step feels uncertain.

REFLECTION QUESTIONS

What is one area where you are clinging to certainty, and how is it holding you back?

How would your life change if you chose growth over comfort?

What steps can you take today to trust yourself more in uncertain situations?

Chapter 2: When Dreams Are Not Enough

When was the last time you questioned the dreams, you were chasing? Were they yours, or had they been handed to you, dressed up in ambition and coated in expectations?

Dream big. Chase the impossible. Make your dreams so massive they scare you.

Yes, it's the kind of message plastered on motivational posters, championed in speeches, and woven into self-help books. It's meant to ignite ambition, yet it often leaves people feeling exhausted, overwhelmed, or questioning their worth.

For years, I promoted this narrative too. Like a lemming, I shared it without ever questioning its validity. The lemming myth, though exaggerated, symbolises blind conformity—following the crowd without thought. I had done just that, sharing without questioning, driven more by what others were saying than the pursuit of truth. One quote, in particular, stuck with me, as it has with many others: "The size of your dreams must always exceed your current capacity to achieve them. If your dreams do not scare you, they are not big enough." — Ellen Johnson Sirleaf

At first, it feels profound. It sounds like the rallying cry of someone destined for greatness. I repeated it, passed it along, and encouraged others to live by it. But with time, I started seeing its flaws.

A dream that scares you? That is anxiety wrapped in a motivational bow. It is not inspiration—such dream is defined as a bloody nightmare. It pushes people into a state of unease, making them believe that only the intimidating or unreachable is worth pursuing. Many continue to follow this idea, chasing dreams that leave them restless and drained.

But what about the dreams that feel simple, natural, and nourishing? The dream of creating a loving home. The dream of building a small café in the neighbourhood. The dream of just having a simple cup of tea or coffee every day. The dream of living peacefully, free from unnecessary drama. The dream of smiling each day without stress or pressure. These dreams are not small. They carry deep purpose and meaning. Yet, the world often dismisses them, focusing instead on ambition that feels overwhelming.

Dreams, whether big or small, come with no guarantees. The dream itself is not the delusion. The delusion is believing that dreams, combined with goals and actions, guarantee achievement and success. Reality often has its own plans.

In India, Dhirubhai Ambani began his journey as a gas station attendant before building one of the world's largest companies, Reliance Industries. His story shows how dreams evolve with time and effort but also require adaptability to unexpected challenges.

Hard work and commitment will not guarantee the outcomes imagined, and that is part of life's unpredictability. Dreams are stepping stones, not destinations. They show you where to begin, but the journey often leads to unexpected places.

There are moments when dreams remain unfulfilled. This never means you have failed. It simply means life has taken its own course. Dreams are possibilities, not certainties. They flow like rivers, sometimes gently, sometimes forcefully, but never in a straight, predictable path.

EXPLORATION TIME
What can you do about dreams?

Acknowledge the pressure you have felt to dream bigger than necessary. Reflect on how this pressure has shaped your choices and whether it truly aligns with your values.

Accept that meaningful dreams never need to overwhelm you. Recognise that true fulfilment often comes from exploration, not intensity.

Identify the dreams that feel natural and fulfilling, not just impressive. Consider what dreams bring you peace and a sense of inner alignment, even when they seem ordinary.

What excites you deeply, even if it seems small? Take a step today—however tiny—toward a dream that feels authentic, not driven by external pressure.

Here is what I've learned: Dream big if that excites you. Dream small if that brings you joy. The size of your dream is not the measure of its worth. What matters is how it shapes you, guides you, and aligns with the life you wish to live. When dreams feel like they are not enough, remember that the true value dwells in the journey—the growth, resilience, and lessons that come along the way.

And what if you have no dreams? If forcing yourself to dream feels exhausting, then stop. Relax. Let go of the pressure to create something that does not feel natural. Life has a way of unfolding in its own time. What is meant to be will find its way to you—with or without a dream. Trust the flow and allow yourself the grace to simply be.

Dreams never need to scare you to be worthy. Whether grand or quiet, the worth of a dream

rests in how it inspires you to live a wholesome, authentic, and meaningful life.

REFLECTION QUESTIONS

What is a dream you have been chasing out of expectation rather than personal desire?

How would your life change if you honoured simpler, more meaningful dreams?

What step can you take today to reconnect with a dream that brings you peace?

Chapter 3: Get Out of Your Comfort Zone? Really?

You've heard it. I've heard it. We've all heard it. "Get out of your comfort zone!"

It's the go-to phrase of motivational speakers, managers, personal trainers, leaders, teachers, parents, and that one overly enthusiastic friend. It's painted as the magic solution to every problem ever.

But what if it is not? What if this overused mantra is not the golden key to growth but a reckless oversimplification?

And yes, I have been guilty of saying it too. I passed it along like a nugget of wisdom—until I realised how sabotaging, anxiety-inducing, and utterly reckless it really is.

Being in your comfort zone is not a flaw. It's a human necessity. Every species on this planet craves comfort. It's what keeps us safe, secure, and sane. Without it, we aren't just stressed—we're at risk of breaking ourselves physically, mentally, and emotionally.

Growth never comes from abandoning your comfort zone entirely. Growth comes from gently stretching it. Imagine lifting weights at the gym. You will not start with 200 kilograms on your first day. You'd begin with something manageable, building strength incrementally. The same applies to personal growth. You expand your comfort zone step by step, not by tearing it apart.

In Japan, Kaizen—a philosophy of continuous, incremental improvement—demonstrates that sustainable growth comes from small, manageable steps rather than drastic leaps. This approach is widely adopted in personal development and business worldwide.

For many, living outside their comfort zone is not a choice—it's their brutal painful reality. Survivors of abuse or those in war-torn environments live daily in the anarchy of uncertainty. Suggesting they "get out of their comfort zone" is not just absurd—it's deeply insensitive. For these individuals, entering a space of safety, security, or love would be the ultimate blessing.

The real problem with "get out of your comfort zone" is its recklessness. It encourages leaps without preparation, equates discomfort with progress, and often leads to burnout. What works instead is expanding your comfort zone intentionally, one step at a time. Do something that feels slightly challenging yet achievable—a stretch, not a strain.

Take Alex Honnold, the world-famous free climber, as an example. He did not start by scaling El Capitan without ropes. Years of preparation, practice, and incremental challenges expanded his capabilities to extraordinary levels. True growth lies in the stretch zone, where challenges push you just enough to inspire growth without tipping into overwhelm.

EXPLORATION TIME
How can you start expanding your comfort zone without overwhelming yourself?

Acknowledge the moments when you have been pressured to leap recklessly into discomfort. Recognise how that pressure may have impacted your sense of safety and balance.

Start small. Speak up in a meeting if that feels slightly uncomfortable. Learn a skill you've been avoiding. Reflect on how each step felt and what it taught you.

Expand intentionally. Growth is a marathon, not a sprint. Trust that small, consistent actions build lasting confidence and strength.

Here's what I have learned: Growth does not require you to abandon comfort or throw yourself into chaos. It requires you to stretch it, gently and consistently, with patience and self-compassion, trusting that steady progress shapes lasting transformation.

Yes, there are times when life forces us out of our comfort zones, and this is when equanimity becomes essential. Imagine being told you are no longer needed at your job. Not politely, not gently—just a cold, clinical email or meeting that takes no account of the years you gave or the plans you built around that stability.

It creates a fear that can easily knock you to the floor, a fear that keeps kicking and punching you until you feel like giving in to the ways of an unwholesome world.

You question everything—your worth, your choices, your future. The old comfort zone—safe, predictable, maybe even dull—is gone, and no amount of clinging will bring it back.

This is where equanimity steps in, not to magically fix it or make it better, but to help you stand your ground amidst the storm. It lets you feel the pain, the anger, and the fear without collapsing into them.

And slowly, step by step, you move forward—not because it is easy or inspiring but because staying down hurts even more. Equanimity holds your hand and embraces you while you walk through the pain and suffering.

Comfort zones are not cages—they are launching pads for sustainable growth.

REFLECTION QUESTIONS
When have you felt pressured to leave your comfort zone in a way that felt unsafe?
What small, intentional step could you take this week to expand your comfort zone?
How has staying within your comfort zone supported your well-being and growth in the past?

Chapter 4: You Are Not Broken, You Are Human

Have you ever felt like you are shattered beyond repair? Like the cracks run so deep they could never be pieced together.

Life has a way of pulling us into this space. Disappointments pile up. Mistakes cling to us. People and situations push us to the edge. And somewhere in all this, a thought creeps in—maybe you are broken.

The Rs tease you—rejection, resentment, and regret. They whisper cruelly in your ear, reminding you of every time you were not enough, every opportunity that slipped away, every person who let you down. They press against your chest, making it hard to breathe, hard to think clearly.

They pull at your mind, replaying moments you wish you could undo, conversations you wish you had handled differently. And just when you think you can move forward, they yank your back, taunting you with their weight, daring you to rise despite them.

∞

Here's the truth: You are not broken. You are human.

There is a practice in Japan called kintsugi. It is the art of repairing broken pottery with gold, making the cracks part of the design. The imperfections are not hidden—they are celebrated. The object becomes more beautiful because it has been through something.

You carry your own golden seams. Those heartbreaks, the struggles, the doubts—they are not proof that you are damaged. They are proof that you've lived, loved, and dared.

Somewhere along the way, the world started selling the idea that perfection is the goal. You see it everywhere—on screens, in conversations, in the curated lives people project. And it is a terrible fatal lie.

∞

The Zulu philosophy of Ubuntu— "I am because we are" —emphasizes community and shared humanity. It teaches that even in brokenness, we find strength through our connections with others.

Life is messy. It is chaotic. It is full of sharp turns, missteps, and imperfections. Being human is about embracing all of it—the joy and the pain, the clarity and the confusion.

Fragility is not weakness. It is life. It means you care. It means you have been open to the world, even when it felt heavy. And that is a strength many will never have.

The scars you carry are not burdens—they are stories. They are proof that you have weathered storms and come out on the other side. They are the quiet whispers of your courage, the testimony of a spirit that refuses to give up.

When you were a child, you may have fallen and scraped your knee. It hurt, yes, but it healed. And now, you likely carry no memory of that pain—only the lesson it left behind. Life works in much the same way. The pain, the doubts, the struggles—they leave marks, but they also leave wisdom. They teach you to stand taller, to trust yourself more deeply.

Society's obsession with perfection has robbed us of this wisdom. It tells us to hide our flaws, to filter our lives into tidy squares, to pretend we have it all figured out. But what if those cracks, those so-called imperfections, are the very things that connect us? What if they are the bridge between your story and mine?

EXPLORATION TIME
What could you do about the lies about being broken?

Acknowledge the cracks you have been hiding from the world. Reflect on how they have shaped you and the strength they represent.

Embrace your scars as part of your story, not something to be concealed. Each mark is a testament to your resilience and growth.

Share your story with someone you trust. Let your vulnerability foster deeper connection and remind others they are not alone.

You are not something to be fixed. You are a story unfolding. Your cracks and scars are not flaws—they are chapters. The world may never fully understand the weight you carry, the battles you fight quietly, the moments you rise when everything inside you feels like falling. And that's okay. You do not owe anyone an explanation.

Let's look at it this way: your DNA—your code, your blueprint—is yours alone. Billions of people on this planet, and not a single one of them has what you do. Even identical twins, born with nearly the same DNA, live lives so different that their stories cannot be swapped. DNA mutates. It adapts. It carries imperfections. And those so-called "flaws" are the reason life even exists. No mutations? No evolution. No change. No strength.

So, when life hits you—when it breaks you open and leaves you raw—remember this: your cracks are not mistakes. They are proof that you have been through hell and kept going. They are the evidence that nothing, not rejection, not regret, not failure, has beaten you yet. You are not broken. You are becoming. You are alive. That is not something to fix—that is something to own and celebrate.

You are never truly alone on this journey. Every step is shaped by the people around you—those who walk beside you, those who came before, and those who will come after.

Your story is yours, but it is connected to the shared experience of everyone you meet. You are not broken. You are whole. You are becoming.

REFLECTION QUESTIONS
What past experiences have shaped you in ways you once saw as flaws but now recognise as strengths?
How can you embrace your vulnerabilities as part of your authentic self?
What steps can you take to share your story more openly and inspire others with your journey?

Chapter 5: You Are Not the Average of the Five People Around You

"You are the average of the five people you spend the most time with."

Jim Rohn's quote has echoed through motivational talks, social media captions, and self-help books, treated as if it holds the ultimate truth about personal growth. But let us take a moment—was it ever true? Or has it always been an oversimplification wrapped in good intentions?

The idea sounds neat. Hang out with the "right" people, and you will magically rise to their level or even higher. But life has never been that simple. Human growth is too intricate to be reduced to a formula about proximity.

To suggest your worth depends solely on who you are around ignores the depth of individual journeys, values, subconscious conditioning, deep-seated traumas, perceptions, and experiences.

Yes, the people around you influence you. Guru Nanak's timeless wisdom, "Sangat buri bura kardande," reminds us of the power of company—how unwholesome associations can lead us astray.

But here is the nuance: Guru Nanak's teachings were never about exclusion or judgment. He never dismissed anyone, no matter how unwholesome their actions might have been. Instead, he encouraged reflection and intentionality—not out of fear, but out of clarity.

The truth is, relationships influence us, and their power lies not in proximity to success but in alignment with our values. An acquaintance of mine, Simone de Haas, offers a refreshing lens on this idea, emphasising the importance of living by our values rather than obsessing over the people we associate with.

She highlights that true growth comes from centring on what guides and grounds us—such as authenticity, respect, care, and creativity. The people we connect with most meaningfully are those who reflect, challenge, and amplify what matters to us. Growth is not about standing next to brilliance; it is about relationships that encourage us to shine our own light.

In Africa, the concept of Harambee, meaning 'pulling together,' reflects the power of collective action. However, it also shows that individual growth thrives when values are aligned with the group's purpose, not just its achievements.

EXPLORATION TIME
What can you do about the lies around personal influence?

Identify your top five values— for example courage, respect, compassion, curiosity, integrity. Reflect on why these values are important to you and how they have shaped your life choices so far.

Next, examine your closest relationships with honesty. Consider how these connections have influenced your sense of self and your personal growth. Assess whether these relationships align

with your values and support the person you strive to become.

Reflect on whether they encourage you to live by your values or create tension that pulls you away from your true self.

This is not about judging or dismissing people. It is about recognising the connections that nourish your spirit versus those that drain it. Some relationships energise, some are neutral, and others may drain you. The goal is not to cut ties but to intentionally nurture what energises and uplifts you.

Think about Jane Goodall. Her connection with Louis Leakey was not about proximity to a famous anthropologist; it was about shared passion and vision. Their relationship amplified her purpose, transforming her journey into something extraordinary. Growth comes from alignment, not status.

Next time someone tells you, "You are the average of the five people around you," smile and remember:

growth is not a formula. It is a practice of living your truth, cultivating meaningful connections, and becoming the person you aspire to be.

You are the embodiment of your values—a versatile, flexible, adaptable, and vibrant mosaic of your journey, and a testament to the power of simple living.

REFLECTION QUESTIONS
What values do you hold most deeply, and how do they shape your relationships?
How have past relationships influenced your personal growth, positively or negatively?
What steps can you take to cultivate relationships that align with your core values?

Chapter 6: Life Promises Nothing, Life Has No Guarantees

Have you ever done everything right, yet the outcome still felt unfair? Witnessed hard work, brilliance, and kindness go unrewarded while arrogance and entitlement thrived?

Throughout my life, I have witnessed individuals with high degrees of laziness, focus, greatness, ruthlessness, and entitlement achieving success. Interestingly, I have also seen people with the same traits fail spectacularly. This paradox reveals an unsettling truth: effort and results are not always walking hand in hand. Hard work, smart strategies, or sheer determination? Sometimes they pay off; sometimes, they will not. Life's outcomes refuse to conform to any kind of neat equation or formula.

Society loves to paint success as predictable. "Put in the work, and the rewards will follow," they say. Yet, life is not a vending machine. You cannot choose your reward simply because you inserted the "right" coin of effort.

Hitting rock bottom does not guarantee an extraordinary comeback. Most of the times, rock bottom is just… rock bottom. Even in moments of raw authenticity, knowing what truly matters, and giving everything you have, success is not guaranteed.

The only certainties in life are being born, living somehow, and eventually dying. Everything else? Infinite possibilities and outcomes, none of which come with promises.

This unpredictability is not a flaw of life; it is its true essence. And the sooner we embrace this, the freer we become. Oh yes! till date I am resisting to embrace and I am getting better at embracing it. Funny how life's unpredictability starts to feel like an old friend, the kind you secretly roll your eyes at but cannot help inviting over for tea.

The fixation on results entangles us in a relentless obsession. Education systems, viral media, and toxic "manifestation" trends glorify outcomes, turning them into measures of our worth. We cling to success as if it were a birthright, believing it defines us. When life refuses to deliver, we crumble under the weight of frustration and blame.

The Bhagavad Gita offers a profound perspective on this dilemma. Lord Krishna's words to Arjuna echo timeless wisdom: "You have a right to perform your prescribed duties, but you are not entitled to the fruits of your actions." This wisdom echoes globally, reminding us to focus on the journey rather than guarantees. In essence, give your best to the task, but release the entanglement of attachment to the outcome, the result. This is not an invitation to apathy; it is a call to freedom—freedom from the anxiety of control.

EXPLORATION TIME

What could you do as life offers no guarantees?

Accept that effort and outcome will not always correlate. Let go of the belief that success is a reward for effort. Focus instead on integrity, learning, and the process itself.

Challenge the idea that failure defines you. Failure is not a permanent label. It is a moment—one that reveals strength and character when faced with courage.

Release the need for certainty. Trust that doing your best today is enough. The future will unfold as it must, regardless of your attempts to control it.

Here is the beauty: when you let go of the fear of failure or the pressure of success, you often perform better. You free yourself to act with courage and clarity, unshackled by the weight of expectation.

Success is not always earned. Failure is not always deserved. Both are shaped by layers of karma, timing, privilege, subconscious conditioning, and countless unseen variables. Effort is like planting a seed. You nurture it with care, ensuring it gets sunlight and water. But the sprouting? That is life's mystery. The joy lies in tending to the garden, not in forcing the bloom. Focus on the process, on the art of giving your best.

Life, like a river, flows unpredictably. Some stretches are gentle, others, turbulent. You cannot command the current, but you can learn to navigate each moment as it comes. This is where resilience lives: not in controlling the river but developing your ability to adapt.

Life promises nothing. It just...is.

REFLECTION QUESTIONS
How has the belief in guaranteed success affected your personal expectations?
In what ways can you shift your focus from outcomes to the experience itself?
What steps can you take to embrace uncertainty while staying committed to personal growth?

Chapter 7: The Beauty of Falling Apart

One day, Ms. Y said to Mr. X, "You're an unhappy person." He paused, took a deep breath and with tears in his eyes simply replied, "Yes." No defence, no excuses—just a quiet acknowledgment of the weight he carried.

And that's where the beauty lies.

Falling apart does not feel beautiful. It feels messy, ugly, painful. It strips away all pretence, leaving you bare and raw. But it is in those raw moments that you truly meet yourself. Like a tree that sheds its leaves in winter, you let go of what no longer serves you, creating space for new growth.

Life will never promise a miraculous turnaround after a collapse. It is in this stillness, this seemingly final place, that reflection and transformation begin. A place where you can sit, reflect, and slowly rebuild— not into the person you were before, but into someone new, someone wiser, someone more whole.

In Sri Lanka, the ancient city of Anuradhapura was rebuilt after being abandoned for centuries, symbolizing resilience and renewal in the face of destruction. True strength is quiet. It shows up in the smallest acts—getting out of bed, making a meal, showing up even when it feels pointless. Resilience is persistent. It never looks glamorous. It looks like failing and trying again, crying and carrying on, breaking and still moving forward.

EXPLORATION TIME
Ever wonder, what possibly you do when you feel like you're falling apart or have fallen apart?

Acknowledge the pain you are experiencing instead of resisting it or repressing it. Let yourself feel without judgment—it is part of healing.

Take small steps toward recovery. Journaling, speaking to a trusted friend, or simply allowing yourself to rest can be profound acts of self-care.

Seek growth in the struggle. Let the discomfort guide you toward self-awareness, patience, and a deeper understanding of your inner strength.

Authenticity is embracing your shadows. It is not about pretending the pain is not there; it is about walking alongside it, learning from it, and using it to shape the path ahead.

When life shatters you, it is not a betrayal—it is a reformation. Some would say it is like a phoenix rising from ashes, falling apart clears the way for something greater. You are not returning to what was; you are creating what can be.

Rebuilding is not a linear process. It begins with small steps: journaling your thoughts, seeking a friend's counsel, or simply finding the courage to wake up and to give it another shot. It is in these actions that the foundation of resilience is laid.

Consider the city of Hiroshima, rebuilt after devastation into a symbol of peace and resilience. Or the practice of pruning a tree to allow for healthier growth. Falling apart is never about surviving—it's about creating something meaningful from the rubble.

Each time you fall, each time you crumble, remember: You are not failing. You are becoming. The process is cyclical, like a spiral—each turn brings you closer to the core of who you are, stronger with every revolution.

Every mark, every scar carries a story of resilience. They whisper lessons about survival, courage, and the power of becoming something new through life's hardships. And here is the truth: Mr. X is me, and Ms. Y is a very, very dear love, who at times can come across as harsh yet has always lifted me up when I no longer wish to get up.

The world often tells us to hide imperfections under the guise of perfectionism, but real beauty lies in the raw and unpolished truths of life. So, let your scars be symbols of strength. Let them reflect the courage it took to rebuild, the wisdom you gained, and the love you discovered for yourself along the way.

Falling apart is not a failure—it is an invitation to rebuild. Each time you do, you create a masterpiece shaped by experience, courage, and the determination to begin anew.

REFLECTION QUESTIONS
When have you experienced personal collapse, and how did you begin to rebuild?
What lessons have your struggles taught you about yourself?
How can you embrace vulnerability as part of your personal growth?

Chapter 8: Everyone Loves Success, ROI in Failure

They say success has a billion admirers, but failure? Yet, behind the sting of failure lies its unmatched power to transform.

By the way, who are these "they" anyway? These mysterious "they" keep showing up uninvited, handing out wisdom like cheap party favours. WTFalafel, WTHummus, WTPickles—what is up with these "they"?

Failure is life's unsparing teacher, stripping away ego and exposing truths. It forces us to ask questions success often disguises: What did not work? Why? What needs to change? And while it stings, it also clarifies. Failure illuminates' paths we never considered and breaks barriers we never dared to challenge.

Consider Dr. C.V. Raman, the first Asian to win a Nobel Prize in Physics. His groundbreaking discovery of the Raman Effect came from countless experiments, many of which failed spectacularly. Yet, each misstep clarified his understanding, leading him closer to success. Failure was not a setback for him; it was a necessary step forward.

Think about the Tata Group in India. After the Nano car—marketed as the world's cheapest car—initially failed to capture the market, the company reevaluated its strategy. They identified key missteps, including poor branding and marketing, and used those lessons to innovate and reposition their approach. The Nano's failure became a stepping stone for broader innovations.

Now, let's talk about the ROI of failure — return on investment. Every failure yields something valuable. The return on failure is profound. Each experience refines your skills, strengthens emotional resilience, and brings clarity about what truly matters. This is how failure transforms from punishment into an invaluable investment in growth.

When you embrace failure's ROI, it stops being a punishment and becomes an investment in growth.

Dr. A.P.J. Abdul Kalam, India's 'Missile Man,' faced early career setbacks but turned them into lessons that propelled his innovations. His failures became the stepping stones to his legacy as a scientist and leader.

In my own life, failure has been both a painful disruptor and a generous teacher. Years ago, I sabotaged a cherished relationship through insecurity and fear. At the time, it felt like an irreversible loss. But through reflection, compassion, and a willingness to learn, that failure taught me the importance of vulnerability and trust. It was a lesson I could not have learned any other way.

EXPLORATION TIME
Eureka time, what can you do when failure stings?

Acknowledge the pain it brings without letting it define you. Failure hurts, but it never makes you unworthy.

Reflect deeply on the experience. Ask yourself: What did not work? What could have been done differently? Seek the insights hidden within the discomfort.

Redefine failure as feedback or better still feedforward. Let the lessons refine your approach, guiding your next steps with clarity and wisdom.

Failure and success are not even ours. We inherit their definitions—passed down through centuries, beaten into us by the systems we are born into. This has been happening for ages, so long that it feels like part of our DNA. Intellectually, some of us get it. We see that failure is just a concept, a story society tells us. But knowing this does not stop us from carrying it like a curse. We dress it up with pretty names like feedback, feedforward, or learning, but the truth is, we drag the same heavy burden. We still label ourselves as failures because that is what we have been taught to do.

Look at how early it starts. A kindergarten classroom: one child gets a shiny star sticker for doing well, and the one who struggles gets nothing. Right there, the message is loud and clear—"You are only worthy if you succeed." That one star? It might as well be a brand. The kids who get nothing begin to feel like nothing. Families, schools, institutions, society—they keep feeding us this same garbage. Success gets the rewards, the praise, the recognition. Struggle? Effort? Resilience? Nobody cares about those. If you do not win, you are invisible.

This is the world we have built. A system where falling short means you are broken, where stumbling once defines your worth forever. And instead of fighting back, we swallow it. We label ourselves as failures because that is the story we have been force-fed for generations.

It is no wonder we pass this poison on to our children. We very rarely teach them that life is learning—that joy, pain, and even destruction is all part of growth. We teach them to fear mistakes, to chase perfection, and to hate themselves when they fall short. And this cycle? It will keep going unless we tear it apart.

Failure is not the problem. The way we have been conditioned to see it is. It is time to stop lying to ourselves and to the next generation. Failure is not the end. It is the raw, ugly, necessary truth that shapes us into something stronger. But only if we let it.

Failure is not an obstacle—it is an investment, many times a bitter one. Learn from it, grow through it, and let it guide you to new heights. Failure demands that we confront our shadows—not to wallow in them but to grow through them. It is about asking tough questions, making difficult changes, and ultimately emerging stronger. It is not about perfection; it is about progress.

So, the next time failure knocks at your door, never slam it shut. Invite it in. Ask it what it has to teach you. Offer it a seat at the table. Because if you listen, failure might just hand you the blueprint for your next breakthrough.

Failure is not the enemy; it is the uninvited guest who lingers awkwardly, messes up your plans, forces you to face the chaos, and leaves behind wisdom—whether or not it leads you to success.

REFLECTION QUESTIONS
What has failure taught you that success never could?
How can you redefine failure as feedback in your current challenges?
What step can you take today to turn a recent failure into a lesson for growth?

PART II: Relationships, Intimacy, and Identity

Before we dive into the messy, beautiful, and transformative world of relationships, let us pause. Part I was a deep dive into self-discovery—the raw truths, the insecurities, and the courage to embrace impermanence. But what good is all this self-awareness if it does not reflect in how we connect with others?

Part II stands as the bridge. It takes everything we unearthed about ourselves and asks us to bring it into the intimate space of connection—where our growth is tested, expanded, and sometimes unravelled. Relationships, after all, are the ultimate testing ground for everything we believe about love, identity, and belonging.

This is where the internal meets the external, where the self-encounters the other. As we step into this section, we shift from looking inward to exploring how we interact with the world around us—through love, intimacy, and shared vulnerability.

Relationships are beautiful. And yes, damn awkward and somewhat chaotic. They hold the potential to lift us to unimaginable heights and also challenge every ounce of our patience and vulnerability. Love, intimacy, family—they carry a promise of connection, yet they demand something raw and honest from us in return.

We dream of connection, crave intimacy and long to be understood. Yet, relationships often show us our darkest corners, the parts of ourselves we hide even from ourselves. We are told that love will complete us, that intimacy will soothe our loneliness, and that family will always be our safe haven.

Wake up and smell the coffee. Love does not erase insecurities—it highlights them. Intimacy is not just about closeness; it is about being brave enough to be truly seen. And family? It can feel like both a sanctuary and a battlefield, often on the same day.

And speaking of impermanence, have you ever thought about how it might be the perfect excuse to dodge commitment? "Why put a label on this when nothing is permanent anyway? Let's just flow with the Tao of 'seeing other people.'" Of course, that's only funny until someone actually takes you seriously and flows right out of your life.

Let's also talk about this idea of unconditional love—a term thrown around like confetti at weddings but rarely backed by reality. Unconditional love sounds poetic. It is absurd unrealistic expectation packaged as romance. Human love comes with conditions, restrictions and the simple fact that we are all human, not saints. The sooner we embrace this truth; the sooner we can navigate relationships with clarity and compassion instead of resentment and disappointment.

We are not here to romanticize relationships or glorify them as battles to conquer. Let's call them what they are: loving, exciting, joyful, transformative, and ridiculous. Love is no magical fix; it's the mirror that shows us who we really are—in all our glory and madness.

You will find reflections on intimacy that transforms, love that heals and hurts, and identity that shifts with the people who come and go in your lives. Together, we will untangle the beauty and awkwardness of relationships—not to fix them, but to appreciate them as part of our journey.

Welcome to Part II: Relationships, Intimacy, and Identity. Let us begin.

Chapter 9: When Love Hurts: Intimacy and Reality

1 Corinthians 13:4–8a (ESV) says: Love is patient and kind; love does not envy or boast; it is not arrogant or rude. It does not insist on its own way; it is not irritable or resentful; it does not rejoice at wrongdoing but rejoices with the truth.

Beautiful, isn't it? But let us be honest: how often does real love look like that? Most of the time, love is messy, exhausting, and full of irritable and resentful moments. Sure, we want love to be patient and kind, but real love? Real love shows up late, drinks the last of the coffee, and leaves you wondering why you signed up for this in the first place.

Love hurts. Not in the poetic way your favourite sad song describes, but in the raw, gut-punching reality that love is not always gentle. It challenges you, pushes you, and makes you confront every part of yourself you have been avoiding. And intimacy? That is no magical fix either. Intimacy is like handing someone a magnifying glass and saying, "Here, take a closer look at all my cracks and scars." Vulnerable? Yes. Uncomfortable? Absolutely.

And then there is that overused phrase: "love conquers all." Spoiler alert: Love thrives not through force, but through harmony and presence. Real love takes courage, honesty, and the ability to admit when you have been a complete jerk. It is not about grand gestures; it is about showing up, even on the days when you would rather not.

Sometimes love feels like a warm embrace. Other times, it feels like a boxing match where neither of you remembers why you started fighting in the first place. And then there are the moments—the raw, soul-crushing moments—when love makes you question everything. Your choices. Your partner. Yourself.

Human love is rarely unconditional, despite the romanticised ideals we cling to. Whether it is the love of a partner, a friend, a parent, or even family, conditions often exist—spoken or unspoken. We expect loyalty, honesty, or reciprocity, and when those expectations break, pain follows. This does not make love any less real; it makes it human. Unconditional love may exist in rare spiritual contexts, but most human relationships carry the weight of conditions—and that is okay, as long as those expectations are clear and healthy.

Here is the thing: Love, in its essence, is not difficult. It is our conditioning, attachments, and expectations that make it seem so. Love hurts because of our fantasy expectations. The nature of love strips away the pretence and demands your authenticity. And while that is terrifying, it is also the most human thing you can do.

Loving hurts. It challenges, frustrates, and sometimes breaks us open. Yet, through that pain, it gives us something irreplaceable—a connection that makes us feel alive, even in the hardest moments. Because love, in all its raw imperfection, is what makes life worth living.

As Rumi said: "Your task is not to seek for love, but merely to seek and find all the barriers within yourself that you have built against it."

Love is not something to chase. It is already in you, but you bury it under walls—fear, ego, and the endless fantasies of how it should be. Love hurts because it strips you bare. It reveals the mess you hide, the wounds you carry, and demands you face them.

The pain of love is not love's fault. It is ours. We cling to what we think love should look like and crumble when it does not. Love does not complete you—it exposes you. And that is terrifying. But it is also the most real thing you will ever feel.

Even if no one loves you, it is okay. As humans, we naturally seek the warmth of connection because we are deeply interdependent. Yet, your value is not defined by the love you receive but by the love you hold within and share with the world.

You can still love someone else, even if you are struggling to love yourself. The notion that you must fully love yourself first is a myth. Love is not a linear process; it flows in many directions, and sometimes, loving others helps you rediscover the love within yourself.

When you care for someone, even while battling your own demons, you step outside your pain. Their presence, their struggles, their humanity remind you that you are not alone. You might forgive their flaws yet hold yours against yourself. Why? Love does not demand perfection from others—so stop demanding it from yourself.

But here is the truth: struggling to love yourself can make you vulnerable. It opens the door to avoidant relationships, where someone keeps their distance, feeding your belief that you are hard to love. It can also make you a target for narcissists, who take and take, convincing you that love is something you have to earn. Loving others while wrestling with your self-worth is brave, but it demands awareness.

Learn to know the difference between love that grows you and love that drains you. I speak from experience—I have seen and felt both. Love that grows you respects you. It does not cling to you or push you away—it gives you space but does not leave you hanging. It communicates, even when it is awkward or tough. It shows up, not just when it is convenient but when it really matters. It is truthful and vulnerable—no masks, no games. It connects in a way that makes you feel like you are seen, heard, and valued.

Love that drains you is the opposite. It ignores your space and makes you feel having your space is a crime. It suffocates you with neediness or keeps you at arm's length with cold indifference. Conversations? Either explosive arguments or complete silence. Vulnerability? Forget it—it hides behind charm, lies, or excuses. It leaves you doubting your worth and wondering why you are the only one trying.

Love that grows you is not perfect, but it makes room for you to be yourself. It challenges you; it fights you but it never asks you to shrink or fade to make someone else comfortable. Love that drains? It thrives on your insecurities and makes you believe it is all your fault.

I have lived both and let me tell you: growing love changes you. Draining love breaks you. One breathes life into you; the other sucks it out. And yes, the growing love has departed from my life. It has transformed into what the world likes to label as "spiritual." Most people say to cling to it, hold tight— out of fear, because letting it go feels like losing something irreplaceable.

But here is the truth: love, even when it leaves, stays with you. It never disappears; it becomes part of you, shaping how you grow, how you heal, and how you love again. Fear tells you to hold on. Growth teaches you to let it be.

The bottom line? Love that grows you lets you breathe, while love that drains will leave you gasping for air.

Love is action, not just feeling. You show up, you care, even when you feel unworthy. And in those moments, something shifts. The cracks inside you start to feel less like failures and more like proof that you are human. Loving someone else while struggling to love yourself is not weakness—it is resilience. But remember this: you deserve a love that builds you up, not one that tears you further apart.

EXPLORATION TIME
Oh!!! this thing called love; how can you deal with it when love feels painful?

Acknowledge the discomfort instead of suppressing it. Pain often signals growth and deeper understanding.

Reflect on your expectations of love and intimacy. Are they rooted in reality, respect, openness or are they fantasies or deep-seated traumas you were taught to believe?

Practice honesty with yourself and your partner. Authentic communication, even when difficult, strengthens connections.

The Sufi poet Rumi often wrote about love's transformative power, describing it as both a source of joy and a crucible for self-discovery. His teachings emphasize that love's challenges lead to inner growth.

So, whether you love yourself first, last, or somewhere in between, just remember love is like dancing to a song you've never heard before—sometimes you step on toes, other times you stumble, but the magic is in showing up and moving to the rhythm anyway. And remember to laugh when you trip.

Just go with the flow… or do your best to avoid entangling yourself in the process. Either way, the enigma of love has a way of keeping things interesting.

REFLECTION QUESTIONS
What beliefs about love have shaped your expectations in relationships?
How can you embrace vulnerability without fearing rejection?
In what ways can love's challenges help you grow emotionally and spiritually?

Chapter 10: Sex: Creation, Connection, and Consequences

For something so human, so universal, it carries more shame, guilt, and societal baggage than it ever should.

Sex is sacred and silly, profound and absurd, exhilarating and awkward. And it's everywhere: in art, religion, locker room whispers, and the occasional regrettable karaoke night.

Let us start with the truth no one tells you. For some, sex is about physical pleasure, for some procreation, and for some both. It's about vulnerability—literally and figuratively. As my father-in-law once told me, it is the naked truth that most shy away from or are too ashamed to face.

It goes beyond baring your body; it's about exposing your insecurities, your desires, and your uncomfortable truths. For something so human, so universal, it carries more shame, guilt, and societal baggage than it ever should.

For centuries, society has tried to control how we talk about sex, who gets to have it, and what "good" sex looks like. Spoiler alert: they've got it all wrong. Whether its purity culture clutching its pearls or unrealistic rom-coms setting up impossibly choreographed bedroom expectations, we've been set up to fail.

The reality? Sex is messy and fun. Sometimes socks stay on. Sometimes there's an unfortunate "oops." And sometimes, the less said about certain moments, the better. And yet, sex is powerful. It creates life—arguably its most primal function—but it also creates connection, trust, heartbreak, and consequences that ripple through lifetimes.

It is an act; it is an exchange of energy, intention, and yes, sometimes regret. It is human in the truest sense of the word. Here's another truth bomb: sex is not one-size-fits-all. For some, it's an expression of love. For others, it's exploration. For some, it's healing; for others, it's Wednesday. Whatever it means to you, it's valid—so long as it comes with honesty and consent.

The Kama Sutra, often misunderstood, is an ancient Indian text that goes beyond physical acts to discuss intimacy, connection, and respect in relationships, showing how sex reflects our humanity.

And speaking of honesty, let us not avoid the elephant in the room—shame. Society has weaponised it for generations. Slut-shaming, virgin-shaming, purity culture—it's all been designed to make you feel inadequate no matter what your choices are. Enough.

The only "wrong" way to approach sex is through deceit, coercion, or harm. Everything else? Your rules, your terms, your journey.

But let us not forget sex is about us as individuals. It's about connection—raw and beautiful connection. It's the shared laughter at an embarrassing moment. The vulnerability of being seen, flaws and all. And yes, sometimes it's about discovering new dimensions of trust, love, or simply joy.

And then, there's the responsibility.

Sex has consequences—health, physical, emotional, mental, even spiritual. It creates life, changes relationships, and leaves marks both seen and unseen. It can shatter trust, destroy lives, and unravel the strongest of bonds. It is a powerful act—a dangerous one when wielded carelessly. The consequences of sex are not always romantic or healing. Sometimes, they are devastating.

EXPLORATION TIME
How can you begin to approach sex with greater wholesome clarity and non-toxic emotional depth?

Reflect on your personal beliefs about sex. Explore how past experiences, cultural messages, and personal values have shaped your understanding of intimacy.

Initiate deeper conversations with your partner. Move beyond surface-level dialogue and explore emotional needs, shields, and what intimacy means to both of you.

Communicate openly with your partner. Share desires, non-negotiables, and expectations with honesty, allowing space for vulnerability and understanding.

Embrace the reality of imperfection. Release societal shame and unrealistic standards around sex. Honour the beauty of vulnerability, humour, and personal growth in your experiences. Ask yourself what ideas about intimacy have shaped your views and whether they align with your current truths.

Recognise that your sexual experiences, needs, wants and desires, when rooted in consent and care, are valid and deeply personal. Sex reflects humanity at its rawest. It exposes our cravings, our fears, our mistakes, and our capacity to create or destroy. Sex is creation, connection, and consequence. It mirrors the beauty and chaos of life itself—messy, vulnerable, and deeply human.

In the end, sex is not about getting it "right." It is about facing its complexities with honesty, care, and the courage to accept both its beauty and its darkness.

The sexual act can bring life, love, and joy, or leave scars that last a lifetime.

∞

REFLECTION QUESTIONS
How have your personal beliefs about sex been shaped by society or upbringing?
What steps can you take to foster open and honest communication in your intimate relationships?
How can you reframe past sexual experiences, both positive and painful, to create a healthier relationship with intimacy?

Chapter 11: Family Bonds: Blood, Distance, and Expectations

Family. The word alone stirs warmth, safety, belonging or pain, pressure, and unresolved tensions that cut deeper than any scar. For some, its warmth, security, and belonging. For others, it's pressure, conflict, and the kind of drama that no reality TV show could script.

They say blood is thicker than water, but that phrase is often misunderstood to mean that family bonds are stronger and more important than any other relationships. However, the actual, original phrase has a different meaning and context:

"The blood of the covenant is thicker than the water of the womb." This actual true version clearly states that the bonds formed by choice, such as friendships or agreements (symbolised by "blood of the covenant"), can be stronger and more significant than those of birth or family (the "water of the womb"). It flips the modern interpretation on its head, emphasising the value of chosen relationships over obligatory ones.

Family bonds are complicated. They're not built solely on genetics but on shared experiences, history, and a lifetime of expectations—many of which are unspoken yet linger heavily, shaping our identities, beliefs, and emotional connections in ways that are often difficult to untangle.

Societal norms often shape these dynamics, pressuring individuals to maintain loyalty despite toxicity and to prioritise blood ties over personal wellbeing. This creates a tension where cultural expectations can obscure the importance of emotional health and personal shields. The concept of Gotong Royong in Indonesia emphasizes communal support, showing that family can extend beyond blood ties to chosen communities.

Let us start with the beauty. Family can be your first home. It's where you learn love, kindness, and the magic of laughter. It's the safety net that catches you when the world feels too harsh. A hug from a parent, a sibling's shared look across the dinner table, or a grandparent's story about the past—these are the moments that make you feel connected to something larger than yourself. But for me, family has been starkly different.

From my younger years and even today, I have longed for acknowledgment, a desire shaped by societal norms that often prioritise obedience over emotional expression. My experience mirrors how unspoken family dynamics can condition us to seek validation in silence, suppressing individuality for the sake of superficial harmony—so many times. My father had a habit of punishing me with silence.

From the age of 10, I can barely recall him speaking to me unless it was to break the silence temporarily, only to return to it when he once again thought and felt I had disrespected him. This pattern defined our relationship. More than half of those years were marked by his silence—a punishment that weighed heavier than words. When I got married, he completely broke communication for approximately 18 years and could not bear the sight of me.

When my drama teacher saw talent in me and requested my family to support my dream of attending drama school, it was met with rejection. Later, when I married my first wife—who was disrespected by my family—we ran away together because there was no room for trust or acceptance. The pain only deepened as I realised my parents often placed their trust in outsiders, society and cultural limitation rather than in me.

Living in a joint family added another layer of complexity. The eldest, so-called caretaker was supposed to guide and protect me but turned out to be a bully. Power-hungry and demanding, he made you feel worthless if you disagreed with him. In that family system, questioning authority meant you were "disrespecting your elders."

Imagine growing up in an environment where questioning was met with contempt, leaving you feeling isolated, unprotected, and deeply untrusting. Over the years, this unwholesome dynamic not only shaped my sense of belonging but also contributed to the cracks that ultimately destroyed my first marriage.

My mother, on the other hand, was affectionate and loving. She gave all the warmth and care she could offer. But the toxicity of the family she married into wore her down, draining her spirit. Over time, she came to accept it as normal—not out of weakness, but out of survival. It was a heartbreaking testament to how deeply ingrained family patterns can damage even the kindest souls, leaving them emotionally exhausted yet still hoping for better.

And yet, amidst all this pain, my former wife and her family have become an unexpected source of healing and still are. Over the years, they showed me a different version of family—one where love does not come with toxic conditions, and disagreements do not turn into lifelong vendettas. Yes, we have our family battles, but they are not carried like revenge stories to the death. There is clarity in our conflicts, knowing that even in the heat of a disagreement, we are still there to support each other. What a contrast, what a way to redefine family.

Family is a paradox. It's both your foundation and your battlefield—rooting you with history and belonging while also being the space where old wounds, expectations, and unresolved conflicts collide. It can ground you, yet it can also weigh you down, making it hard to break free from inherited patterns of pain. And while not every family story is a happy one, every family teaches you something—even if that lesson is simply how to walk away with grace and strength.

At its best, family offers strength, nurturing, and unconditional support—a sanctuary in life's storms. At its worst, it's a maze of obligations, toxic cycles, and unresolved emotions. And yet, even in the chaos, family teaches us to endure, to dream, and to survive. It shapes not only our identity but also our capacity to give and receive love.

EXPLORATION TIME
OMG!!! What can you do to redefine your relationship with family bonds?

Reflect on the unspoken expectations you carry about family and whether they serve your

emotional, mental, physical, financial and spiritual well-being.

Initiate honest conversations with those you trust, aiming for clarity and understanding rather than blame.

Release the need for validation from those who may never provide it—focus instead on building chosen connections that uplift you.

Family, for all its complexity, is where we first understand love—and sometimes, where we first learn heartbreak. But the ache of not belonging, of feeling unseen, cuts the deepest. Healing from family wounds does not mean erasing them.

It means taking intentional steps toward emotional recovery—whether that involves journaling to process your pain, seeking therapy for deeper guidance, or setting healthy shields that protect your peace.

It means acknowledging them, forgiving where you can, and creating the relationships you need for

yourself. Sometimes, healing means letting go—not out of bitterness, but to protect your peace.

Family—the joy, the pain, the heartbreak—stays with us forever because it shapes who we are, etching itself into our soul. A bittersweet melody we carry wherever we go.

REFLECTION QUESTIONS:
How have your family experiences shaped your understanding of love and trust?
What shields, if any, do you need to establish to protect your emotional well-being?
How can you redefine the idea of family in a way that supports your growth and peace?

Chapter 12: They Judge The Handsome Silver Fox

Have you ever been reduced to a label—judged not for who you are but for the surface others see? It is easy to assume judgments are harmless, but they cut deeper than most of us care to admit. Labels are rarely about you; they are reflections of other people's biases, yet we often end up carrying their weight.

Once upon a time, in a land not so far away, a man decided to grow a beard. It was not just any beard; it was the kind that could transform an ordinary mortal into a "handsome silver fox." Or so the tale goes. What he did not anticipate, however, was that this simple act would turn his life into something of a modern-day fable.

Some villagers whispered, "He looks wise, like a sage who could solve all our problems." Others frowned and said, "It is a disaster! Off with the beard!" It seemed everyone had an opinion. From wisdom and gravitas to outright yuckose, the beard evoked everything but indifference. And thus began the saga of the handsome silver fox, a tale not about a beard, but about the strange power of judgement.

∞

By the way, that handsome silver fox? That is me. Erika, the lovely and gorgeous lady, called me that, while some others said I looked scruffy. But I will take what Erika said as the complete truth and nothing but the truth. Lol, lol, lol.

At this point I need to clarify I highly promote proper grooming and hygiene and encourage everyone to always prioritise that.

You are not your clothes. You are not your name. And you are definitely not your skin. But good luck convincing the world of that. The world loves its labels, and it is quick to slap one on you without ever bothering to look beyond the surface. Clothes, names, skin—these are the shortcuts people use to decide whether you belong or not.

Let us start with clothes. Society says, "Do not judge a book by its cover," but then turns around and hands you a wardrobe manual. A suit commands respect; a hoodie invites suspicion. A designer label can get you into places where a worn-out shirt would only get you the door slammed in your face. Unless you are a celebrity, famous or rich individual you will be allowed entrance even if you came to in your undervest.

I am still told to this day that how I dress determines whether people will take me seriously. And then I hear the classic advice: 'Always dress better than everyone in the room, it will impress them.' Well, life is not about impressing others; it is about taking care of yourself. Imagine being a kid, then a teenager and then as an adult, realising that your self-worth, at least in the eyes of others, could be stitched into a piece of fabric. It is ridiculous and suffocating.

Then there is your name. A name is supposed to carry history, identity, celebration. But the wrong name in the wrong place? It becomes a flashing neon sign that screams, "You are different." I have lived the awkwardness of hearing someone butcher my name—not with curiosity but with condescension. The subtle tone that says, "Your name is too hard, too foreign, too much." It is not just about the sound; it is about the dismissal. A name should be a celebration, not an obstacle.

∞

Then there is the skin—the label you cannot take off. Its colour becomes a passport or a barrier, a privilege or a punishment. Society's obsession with categorising people by their skin tone has left scars that run deep. It dictates opportunities, safety, and even humanity itself. I remember moments when I felt scrutinised, not for what I said or did, but for how I looked. It is the kind of judgment that does not just hurt; it wounds.

But judgment is not limited to the big things. It is the smaller, seemingly trivial aspects of our appearance that spark endless opinions. This got me thinking about the assumptions we carry and how they shape our interactions. It also reinforced a truth I hold close: while judgment from others may be inevitable, self-care is non-negotiable. Proper grooming and hygiene are not about meeting anyone else's standards but about respecting and valuing yourself.

If something as simple as facial hair, nail polish, jewellery, phone, the car you drive can evoke strong opinions, imagine the judgments tied to things far more intrinsic, like names or skin colour. These judgments are not about you; they are about the biases of those making them. Yet, you are the one who ends up carrying their weight.

EXPLORATION TIME
Let us introspect, what do you do when the world judges you—and when you find yourself judging others?

Prioritise self-respect above public opinion. Present yourself in ways that align with your values, not society's biases.

Release the need for external validation. Understand that your worth is not determined by how others perceive your clothes, name, or appearance.

Cultivate self-compassion. When unfairly judged, remind yourself of your deeper qualities—kindness, integrity, and resilience.

Pause before judging others. When you catch yourself making assumptions, ask: "What story am I missing?" Challenge yourself to see beyond appearances.

Examine your biases. Reflect on where your judgments stem from—cultural conditioning, personal experiences, or misunderstandings.

Practice empathy. Remember that everyone carries struggles you cannot see. Offer the same grace you wish to receive.

The truth is people will always judge. That is their problem, not yours. Your clothes never define your character. Your name is not a limitation. Your skin is not a boundary. While judgment is inevitable, self-care remains essential. Prioritising proper grooming and hygiene is not about meeting anyone's expectations—it is about respecting yourself and ensuring you present yourself in the best way possible.

I have worn this burden. Judged by my clothes, dismissed because of my name, scrutinised for my skin, critiqued for a beard, the car I drive and the phone I use. These experiences leave marks—some visible, others buried deep. But they also teach resilience. They teach you to stand tall in the face of judgment. In Nigeria, the Igbo proverb, 'A man is not valued where he is born but where he is known,' highlights how perception shapes identity and value in society.

When the world labels you, refuse to let their judgments shrink you. You take the very things they misunderstand and turn them into your strengths. Your clothes, your name, your skin— these are not burdens; they are your story.

REFLECTION QUESTIONS
How have judgments from others shaped your self-image, and how often have you judged others based on appearance?

What personal values can help you rise above external criticism and avoid unfairly judging others?
How can you practice self-respect without seeking validation from others while offering the same grace to those around you?

Chapter 13: The Weight of Expectations

Expectations are like invisible chains, handed down with a smile and wrapped in words like, "We just want what is best for you." Sounds lovely, does it not? But no one ever tells you that what is "best for you" often feels like a noose around the neck. Restrictive. Suffocating. I remember being told to follow the path laid out for me without question—compliance disguised as care. It was as if being loved was tied to meeting a standard I never agreed to in the first place.

As a kid, I was taught you follow the script, or you pay the price. At home, it was all about respect. Questioning elders? That was as acceptable as setting the dining table on fire. School was not much better.

Imagine hating studies and being trapped in a system where the only reward for good behaviour was... more expectations. And when you failed? Humiliation, of course. There was a hierarchy of shame—standing next to your desk, then on the chair, then on the desk itself. And the grand finale? Standing on that desk with a pointed hat that screamed 'DONKEY' in bold letters. The emotional aftermath was not just embarrassment—it planted a quiet fear of failure, a distrust of authority that demanded compliance without understanding. It made me question whether respect was earned or simply demanded through power. Subtle, right? Yes, I experienced this in my years at boarding school.

Being the youngest sibling was its own special kind of hell. Every move I made was compared to my brothers and sister. "Why can you not be more like them?" seemed to be my life's soundtrack. Everything from how I studied to how I walked, even to how I spoke, was judged. Having an opinion was an act of rebellion. "You are too young to understand," they would say. Funny how being too young came with all the responsibility but none of the freedom.

So, what does all this do to a person? It builds resentment. Not the loud, punch-a-wall kind, but the quiet, simmering type that eats away at you. I grew to hate authority—anyone who demanded respect without earning it.

Thus, I have become obsessed with fairness. I will fight for justice even if it means burning myself out in the process. It is not a healthy habit, but when you are raised in a world of "do as I say, not as I do," you cling to fairness like a life raft. This obsession has shaped both my professional and personal choices. In business, I have gone to great lengths to ensure every agreement is transparent and ethical, even when it has cost me financially. On a personal level, it has made me wary of relationships where honesty is compromised, often leading to emotional exhaustion in my efforts to defend what feels right.

Professionally, I am a speaker, someone who thrives on the stage. But personally? Social gatherings make me want to run for the hills. Forming friendships feels like trying to build a bridge while the river keeps rising. Vulnerability is scary. And when friends label you "toxic" for being honest, it reinforces that fear. If you cannot show your cracks to your friends, what is the point of friendship?

Here is a twist. Amidst all this mess, my former wife and her family show me a wholesome expectation. Yes, disagreements happen, but they are resolved without turning into a lifelong war. It is a strange feeling—to be supported without strings attached. It is something I am still learning to trust. In Confucian philosophy, respect for elders and societal roles is emphasized, but so is the importance of personal integrity and questioning unjust expectations.

In my work, expectations have been both a burden and a teacher. For years, I bent over backwards to meet client demands, sacrificing my own financial well-being in the process. The fear of financial instability kept me compliant. But recently, I have started saying no. Not out of arrogance, but because some expectations simply are not worth the cost. I remember turning down a training engagement of ten days where the terms were exploitative in all ways possible. despite the financial strain I was under. It was terrifying, but it marked a turning point where I chose self-respect over compliance. It is liberating to stand by your values, even when the cost feels uncomfortable.

EXPLORATION TIME

What can you do when expectations weigh you down—or when you place them unfairly on others?

Identify the expectations you carry—are they truly yours, or inherited from others? Consider where these beliefs originated and whether they genuinely serve your personal growth today.

Release the need for approval from those who demand your conformity. Remember, your worth is not tied to meeting someone else's ideals but to how you honour your own truth.

Reflect on whether you impose expectations on others. Are they fair, or shaped by your own fears and conditioning? Consider whether your guidance uplifts or limits those around you.

Create space for personal freedom and emotional clarity. Instead of restricting yourself with rigid

demands, give yourself permission to evolve and redefine your identity.

Choose to support others with empathy instead of pressure, focusing on encouragement rather than control. Ask how you can uplift someone without needing them to meet your standards.

Expectations are not inherently harmful, but when they demand you sacrifice your authenticity, they become chains. The weight of expectations will always be present, but the power to carry or release them lies within you. Expectations are not the villain of this story. They can be a guide, encouragement, even a source of inspiration. The trick is learning which ones to carry and which ones to break.

Some expectations can be good. Like expecting yourself to grow, attempting again after failure, or to take care of those you love. But others? They suffocate you. Think of the kid in school who gets nothing while another gets a gold star because they fit the system's idea of "smart." Or the person who's labelled a failure because they don't own a house or

have the "perfect" job by 30. These are the chains—
the ones that crush you and make you feel like you're
never enough.

Here's the thing: you will let people down. Your
parents might not get the career choice they dreamed
of for you. Your friends might not understand your
decisions. And that's okay. The real work is deciding
which expectations to carry and which to let go of.
Carry the ones that inspire you, that push you to
grow. Break the ones that demand you sacrifice who
you are just to make someone else happy. In the end,
it's your life—live it on your terms, not theirs.

***Expectations will always exist, but they lose their
weight when you find the courage to let go of
what was never yours to carry—breaking free
from the invisible chains that once restricted you,
reclaiming the space to live on your terms.***

REFLECTION QUESTIONS

What expectations from your past still shape your choices today?

How can you distinguish between healthy encouragement and restrictive demands?

How do you project expectations onto others, and what can you do to foster healthier connections?

Chapter 14: Childhood Wounds in Adult Hearts

The wounds of childhood are not merely memories; they are echoes that linger in the quiet corners of your mind. You grow older, build a life, and convince yourself you've moved on—but those early scars often show up in your adult heart when you least expect them. A harsh word, a friend's betrayal, a moment of humiliation—once small, now reshaped as fear, doubt, and hesitation.

The truth is, childhood wounds plant seeds that grow into beliefs: "I am not enough," "Love has to be earned," "Trust will get you hurt." These beliefs shape how you see yourself and how you show up in the world. They colour your relationships, your self-worth, and even the risks you take—or avoid.

Take, for instance, the child who was always told to keep quiet. That silence often grows into an adult who fears speaking up, worrying their voice does not matter. Or the child who faced rejection and now carries a constant fear of abandonment, clinging too tightly or pushing people away first. These patterns are not random; they are echoes of pain left unresolved.

I know this intimately. My childhood was marked by moments that shaped me in ways I did not fully understand until adulthood. Being silenced for questioning authority made it difficult for me to express myself later in life without guilt or shame. Being constantly compared to my siblings taught me that my worth was performance-based—that success was the only way to feel valued.

It is easy to think time alone heals these wounds. It does not. Time may dull the sharpness of pain, but without addressing and understanding those wounds, they continue to shape how you move through life— silently influencing your choices and self-perception. Unaddressed pain seeps into your decisions, your relationships, your very identity. For years, I felt the weight of those comparisons and that silence pressing against me, turning achievements into desperate attempts to feel seen and failures into proof of personal inadequacy.

But wounds, as deep as they are, do not have to define you. A scar is not a chain. A scar is a story of survival—a mark not of damage but of resilience, reminding you that you have endured and risen despite the pain. Reframing scars this way transforms them from symbols of victimhood into emblems of empowerment. Nelson Mandela, whose childhood was marked by injustice, transformed his pain into a lifelong commitment to equality and reconciliation. Pain, when met with courage and compassion, can become the foundation of profound strength.

Healing childhood wounds is not about forgetting. It is about facing those moments with courage, naming the pain, and refusing to let it shape your identity any longer. It is about forgiveness—of those who hurt you, yes, but also of yourself. Forgiving yourself for the times you let those old fears hold you back.

Self-compassion is essential in this process, allowing you to approach your healing journey with kindness rather than self-criticism.

EXPLORATION TIME

What can you do to begin healing childhood wounds?

Acknowledge the pain. Name the moments that hurt you. They no longer need to remain hidden.

Identify how they influence your present. Notice where old fears show up—whether in relationships, self-worth, or decisions.

Challenge those beliefs. Ask yourself: "Does this belief truly define me, or was it something I was taught?"

Offer yourself the care you lacked. Speak to yourself with kindness and reassurance, the way you once needed.

Rewrite the narrative. Your pain is a chapter, not the entire story. Choose to define yourself by how you rise, not how you were hurt.

The wounds of childhood can leave lasting imprints, but they do not own you. Healing is not a final destination but an ongoing process, one where each step forward allows you to reclaim more of your strength and authenticity. Your worth was never dependent on those moments. Healing is not about erasing the past; it is about reclaiming your story, recognising your strength, and embracing the courage to move forward.

A wounded heart is not a broken one. It is proof that you have felt deeply, endured, and are still capable of love, growth, and healing.

REFLECTION QUESTIONS
What childhood experiences still influence the way you see yourself today?
How can you begin to challenge old beliefs that no longer serve you?
What acts of self-compassion can you offer yourself to support your healing journey?

Chapter 15: The Shadows of Abuse We Carry

Abuse is not always loud or dramatic. Sometimes, it whispers in the silence, lurking in the spaces where love should have been. Abuse creeps into your life in ways that are hard to name. The harsh words that cut you down, the silence that makes you feel invisible, the hand that strikes, the manipulation that twists your mind, or the violation that shatters your sense of safety. Abuse makes you question your worth, your safety, and even your reality.

The problem with abuse is not just that it hurts, but that it loiters. It seeps into everyday life, manifesting as over-explaining, people-pleasing, difficulty setting shields, and an underlying fear of abandonment. Abuse plants seeds of doubt and fear that can shape your life in ways you never agreed to. It convinces you the pain was your fault when it never was — long after the bruises fade, long after the words stop echoing.

I have experienced abuse—mental, emotional, physical, and sexual. The first time I faced mental abuse; I was too young to understand it. The words, the dismissals, the constant "you're not enough"— they became a script in my mind. The first time I experienced physical abuse; I thought it was my fault. I thought, "If I had just done better, maybe this wouldn't have happened." And then there is the weight of sexual abuse—it tears apart your sense of safety and trust, leaving behind disgust, fear, and a feeling of being shattered.

The pain of abuse makes you build walls so high that even compassion and love find it tough to climb over. Trust has never come easily to me. Abuse made trusting feel like a gamble, as though letting my guard down might invite harm again. Even now, I remain vigilant, knowing that the moment I let my guard of safety down, the patterns of abuse may reappear.

Anyone who has endured abuse is not seeking attention or pity; they are seeking relief. They want the pain, the hurt, the disgust to go away. They want to reclaim the parts of themselves that abuse tried to mutilate and erase.

Abuse stays in the body, the mind, and the heart. Dr. Gabor Maté speaks of how trauma embeds itself deeply, manifesting as physical pain, addiction, or self-sabotage. Abuse convinces you to carry its weight long after it has passed. But it does not have to own you.

Look at Malala Yousafzai. After surviving a near-fatal attack, she transformed her trauma into a global movement for girls' education. Thich Nhat Hanh said it best: "Suffering is not enough. Life is both dreadful and wonderful. We must also be in touch with the wonders of life."

Healing is not linear. Some days the shadow feels lighter, while other days, it clings like a second skin, reminding you that progress can coexist with moments of struggle. Setbacks never mean failure; they are part of the process, allowing you to learn, grow, and strengthen along the way. Healing is not about erasing the shadow but learning to live alongside it—to find light in the cracks.

Humour has been my unexpected ally, helping me reclaim a sense of control over painful memories and shift from despair to resilience. When I look back on some of those painful moments, I do my best not to dwell in self-pity. Instead, I find myself saying, "WTFalafel, that was awful!" And yet, I am still here. These experiences have not turned my heart to stone. They have taught me to use compassion and even humour to ease the weight of the memories. Laughter, for me, is not about dismissing the pain—it is a quiet act of defiance that says, "Even if you break me, I will rise."

Abuse leaves scars, yes. But scars are not signs of weakness. They are powerful reminders of the battles you have faced and survived, shifting your identity from victimhood to empowerment by proving your resilience. They are proof you are still alive. They are the seams of a life stitched back together, stronger at the breaks. Remember kintsugi—the Japanese art of repairing broken pottery with gold—reminds us that your cracks never diminish you; they make you radiant.

EXPLORATION TIME
What can you do when the shadows of abuse linger?

Acknowledge the scars you carry. They are not signs of failure but evidence of survival. Name your pain—it no longer needs to remain hidden.

Recognise the patterns. Notice how past wounds shape your relationships, your trust, and your self-worth. Awareness is the first step toward breaking free.

Release the blame you carry. Abuse was never your fault. The burden belongs to the one who caused the harm, not you.

Seek safe spaces for healing. Whether through therapy, journaling, or sharing your story with someone you trust, give yourself permission to express the pain.

Reclaim your narrative. You are never defined by what happened to you. You are defined by your courage to keep going.

To those still living with the shadows of abuse, know this: healing is not about erasing the past; it means learning to conduct it differently. Your pain is not something to overcome, but something to pass through. You may not always be able to speak it, and that is okay. Healing often begins quietly—with a small act of kindness toward yourself, a moment of recognising the strength it takes to move forward.

You are not required to share your story with anyone; instead, you can offer yourself the patience to process it in your own way. Your existence in itself is a testament to resilience, and that is where your light begins. The scars of abuse remain, yet it can never hold the power to define you. The light will never erase the shadows, yet it guides you toward a place where the weight lessens, allowing you to move freely again.

The marks of abuse leave cast long shadows over your life. Yet, even amidst the darkness, there is a spark within you—a quiet resilience that no shadow can extinguish. This resilience is your light, guiding you to moments of clarity, strength, and freedom.

It is never about erasing the pain but finding ways to let the light grow stronger than the darkness.

REFLECTION QUESTIONS
What past wounds have shaped the way you trust and connect with others today?
What steps can you take to begin releasing the pain and blame that is not yours to carry?
How can you honour your healing journey while embracing the strength your scars represent?

PART III: Work, Growth, and Hustle

Before diving into the demands and realities of work, growth, and hustle, let us pause. Part II explored the complexities of relationships and identity—the ways in which our connections with others reflect, challenge, and shape us. But relationships are not limited to people. They extend to the work we do, the goals we chase, and the ambitions that define us.

Part III is the next step in our journey. It is where the deeply personal meets the societal. It asks us to examine not just how we navigate our internal worlds or our closest bonds, but how we function in a system that glorifies productivity, growth, and relentless hustle.

This is the bridge between the personal and the professional, between what we value internally and how we apply those values in the external world. It prepares us to confront the illusions we hold about work, the lies we tell ourselves about success, and the systems that exploit our need for purpose. In this

section, we will explore not just what we do, but who we become in the process of doing it.

∞

Work. Growth. Hustle. The holy trinity of modern life—or so they say.

Work is a blessing and let me say that again: work *is* a blessing. To create, to contribute, to bring value into the world—what an honour that is. And somewhere along the way, this blessing got wrapped in expectations that no one agreed to. "Treat work like family," they tell us. But here is the thing about family: it comes with unspoken rules, unexpected demands, and a loyalty contract you never signed but are somehow bound by. Sound familiar? Exactly.

Now imagine that dynamic in a workplace. The loyalty, the sacrifice, the late nights—all in the name of being part of something bigger. And here is the reality: when profits need protecting, you are no longer part of the "family." You are a number on a spreadsheet, a line item to cut. Loyalty? It seems to flow in only one direction.

And then there is growth—the dazzling promise of becoming your "best self." Growth gets sold as a straight line, a smooth climb up the ladder. And here is the truth: growth is not a ladder. It is a tangled mess of mistakes, doubts, and moments where you feel like you are going backwards. It is uncomfortable, unpredictable, and never as pretty as the posters make it look. But does it matter? Absolutely. Even when it drags you through the mud.

And finally, hustle—the badge of honour for modern ambition. "Grind harder!" they say. "Sacrifice more!" But hustle culture is not a path to greatness; it is a fast track to burnout. The loudest voices preaching hustle are often the ones who have already "made it," lounging in luxury while the rest of us are stuck in the grind. Hustle does not build dreams. It just keeps you too busy to realise when you are chasing the wrong ones.

So here is the real question: Why are we working, growing, and hustling like this? We are born, celebrated as blessings, yet we find ourselves trapped in cycles of fear, stress, and expectation.

What is the point of being born just to live like this—
and then quietly disappear into the grave? Or, for
those who prefer flames, to be cremated with a folder
of unfinished to-do lists?

In this part, we will strip away the illusions. Work is a
blessing—but it is not your identity. Growth is
messy— but is inevitable. And hustle? It is time to
stop glorifying it and start asking what really matters.
No fluff, no sugar-coating—just honest reflections
about what it really means to navigate work, growth,
and hustle in a world obsessed with shiny illusions.

Welcome to Part III: Work, Growth, and Hustle. Let us
get into it.

Chapter 16: No, Work Is Not Your Family

Work is not a curse, nor is it a burden. It is a blessing. It gives purpose, structure, and a means to contribute to something beyond oneself. Through work, skills sharpen, ideas manifest, and impact takes form. It is how innovation thrives, how communities sustain, and how individuals find their place in the world.

Yet, for all its value, work is not family. No matter how warm the culture, how close the colleagues, or how inspiring the leadership, the workplace is not a home. Work is where value must be proven. Never romanticise it. Family stays when you falter. Work measures performance. One is built on belonging, the other on contribution.

Yes, some workplaces are toxic. Some chew people up and spit them out. Yet even the worst jobs provide something—money, experience, connections, or a wake-up call. Respect that. Never sit in self-pity either. Staying in a place that drains you out of misplaced toughness or because you fear the unknown is not strength—it is self-inflicted stagnation. The outside world is not a fairytale, but it is not a monster either. You can leave. You can start again. You are not a tree.

Appreciate work for what it is—a blessing. But never mistake it for what it is not. Work is not your family. Let us get that straight. It never was, and it never will be.

Still, the myth persists. "We are a family here! Welcome to the family," they declare at onboarding sessions, in motivational emails ad talks, and at those cringe-worthy team-building retreats. And for years, I bought into it. I believed that my loyalty, hard work, and results would solidify my place in the company. I thought, "This is it! A second family." But then came the wake-up call.

I was made redundant. Just like that. Despite being a high performer. Despite giving my all. The decision was political. HR's words? Cold and clear: "It is just business." Turns out, I was not a valued family member—I was a number on a spreadsheet. That moment hit hard. It hurt. It felt like a betrayal, a rupture of trust I had never questioned. But it also woke me up.

Work is not family. A caring family never sends you packing when profits dip or when politics play out. A loving family cares for you when you work those extra hours and late nights. They recognise your effort and appreciate it in ways that truly matter. And a compassionate family definitely never reduces you to a line item in their budget.

Now, let me pause and say this: there are exceptions—those rare, golden stories where companies truly act like family. And I have heard them firsthand. Stories about organisations that stood by their people through the roughest times, that helped employees thrive and even encouraged them to move on to greener pastures when the time was right. And you know what? You can tell these stories are real because of the way people still speak about those companies—with emotion, with gratitude, with a connection that runs deeper than any contract. That is incredible. Hats off to those companies.

And let us not forget the bonds we form along the way. Without a doubt, there will be a few colleagues whose friendships go beyond the workplace. These are the ones you will happily call your extended family—the rare connections that survive resignations, new jobs, and the passage of time. They are the exceptions that make the journey worthwhile.

But for most of us, work is about contracts, agreements, and mutual benefit. And when push comes to shove, the numbers almost always win. This is not a complaint. It is clarity. It is about understanding what work is—and what it is not.

EXPLORATION TIME
What can you do when work blurs the lines of loyalty and identity?

Acknowledge the professional nature of work. Value your role but remember it is a partnership, not a bond of unconditional loyalty.

Invest in yourself beyond your job title. Explore passions, hobbies, and relationships outside the

workplace that bring you personal fulfilment. Your identity is far richer than your career accomplishments.

Redefine loyalty. Stay committed to your work while honouring your personal values and well-being. Loyalty to yourself comes first, never as a sacrifice for someone else's agenda.

Separate validation from professional achievement. Your worth is not defined by job performance or company praise. Who you are extends far beyond how you are seen in professional spaces.

Nurture connections with care. Build friendships at work but understand they thrive when mutual, not forced by corporate culture. True connections are based on shared values, not shared tasks.

Not all workplaces are your family. It is a space of collaboration, exchange, and, sometimes, incredible growth. When you recognise it for what it truly is, you gain the freedom to value it for its purpose—without mistaking it for your core identity.

Work can be fulfilling. It can even be beautiful. And it cannot be everything. As Dr Gabor Maté puts it, "The workaholic often believes they have to justify their existence through productivity because they were never made to feel inherently worthy as a child". They learned that love, approval, and even their sense of self had to be earned. That belief doesn't vanish with adulthood; it grows roots. We convince ourselves that being busy, producing more, and achieving endlessly will somehow fill the void left by those early lessons in conditional worth.

But it never does. Instead, the cycle becomes suffocating. We sacrifice relationships, passions, and even our health chasing the illusion that productivity makes us enough. And when the work is gone—when a redundancy notice lands or burnout takes over—it feels like the ground beneath us disappears, because we've built everything on this fragile foundation. That's where I've been, and I'm still learning the hard way to invest in the things work cannot take away: people I love, passions that light me up, and communities that remind me I am more than my output.

Work is a blessing, not a bondage. Recognise it for what it is, and you will value it even more.

REFLECTION QUESTIONS
Have you ever confused work loyalty with personal identity? What impact did it have?
How can you begin nurturing a fulfilling life outside your professional role?
What values will guide your relationships and commitments at work moving forward?

Chapter 17: Perfection Is Overrated

Perfection. It sounds good, does it not? The shining, unattainable promise.

The illusion sold as the ultimate standard, yet so slippery it dissolves the moment you reach for it. The thing we are all supposed to strive for. But here is the uncomfortable truth: what is perfect to me might be meaningless to you. And what you call perfection could be invisible to someone else entirely.

Think about it. Health? To some, it is chiselled abs. To others, it is simply playing with their kids without running out of breath. Love? For one, it is poetry and roses. For another, it is quiet, steady companionship without the noise. Success? Someone dreams of a mansion on the hill; another just wants a safe space where they belong. So, whose perfection is the right one?

This obsession with perfection is exhausting and, sadly, paralysing. I have seen it in the workplace, time and time again. The perfectionist who polishes and

tweaks endlessly, while deadlines pass and opportunities vanish. Innovation dies under the weight of "It has to be just right." And while perfection waits, the world moves on. The so-called perfect work becomes irrelevant before it is even finished.

Let me be clear: rejecting perfectionism is not the same as rejecting excellence. It is not an excuse to be careless or complacent. This never means we abandon effort or stop aiming high. But there is a difference between striving for excellence and being trapped by perfection. Excellence is about showing up fully, giving your best with the resources you have—without the fear of imperfection chaining you to inaction. Perfectionism kills creativity because it whispers, "If it is not flawless, do not even try."

The greatest innovations, the boldest ideas, the most profound human connections—they were never perfect. They were raw. Messy. Unfinished. And yet, they mattered.

Perfectionism is not just exhausting—it is self-destructive. It fuels anxiety, creates endless self-doubt, and convinces you that nothing is ever good enough. The irony? The more you chase perfection, the less satisfied you feel.

EXPLORATION TIME

What do you do when perfectionism wants to control your life—and when you expect perfection from others?

Redefine success on your own terms. Stop chasing the impossible and focus on meaningful progress, not flawlessness. True success is found in effort and impact, not in unreachable ideals.

Take action before you feel fully prepared. Perfection often hides behind the lie of "I need more time." Begin, even when it feels messy. The courage to start imperfectly is often the first step toward growth.

Value progress over perfection. Small, consistent steps create growth—far more than waiting for the elusive perfect moment. Progress builds momentum, while perfection keeps you frozen.

Embrace mistakes as invitations to grow. Let every mistake become a mirror for learning instead of a mark of failure. Mistakes are not evidence of inadequacy—they are stepping stones to mastery.

Practice compassion when others fall short. If you expect yourself to be perfect, you likely hold others to impossible standards too. Release both. Grace allows room for authenticity, growth, and deeper connection.

Look around you. Nature is filled with imperfection—crooked trees, asymmetrical flowers, clouds without rules. And it is breathtaking. Not because it is flawless, but because it exists, alive and unapologetically unique.

This imperfection is, in itself, perfect. It is the harmony found in a loving relationship where quirks and flaws create intimacy and laughter. It is the spirit of a great workplace where creativity thrives in the messy corners of collaboration and honest mistakes. It is why we look at something beautifully human—

whether a moment, a bond, or a place—and say with awe, It is just perfect. Because perfection does not mean pristine; it means real.

Rejecting perfectionism is not the same as rejecting excellence. Perfectionism keeps you stuck, chasing an impossible ideal, terrified of messing up. Excellence is different—it is about doing your best with what you have, right here, right now. It is not about being flawless; it is about being real.

In a relationship, excellence is not pretending everything is perfect or never arguing. It is showing up, loving hard, and working through the messy stuff together. At work, it is not about being a superstar every second. It is using your knowledge, skills, attitude, time, and resources to create something meaningful, even when the odds are not perfect.

Excellence is about determination, not perfection. It is about knowing what you have—your knowledge, skills, attitude, resources, and time—and using them fully. It is messy, it is human, and it is where the real magic happens.

Perfection is an illusion that keeps you stuck. Life is about being real, showing up, and growing—messy edges and all.

Forget perfect. Embrace the messy, the flawed, and the real—that is where life happens. That is where excellence is born.

REFLECTION QUESTIONS
Where in your life have you delayed action because of the fear of not being perfect?
What would it feel like to measure success based on progress rather than perfection?
How can you begin showing yourself and others more grace in the face of imperfection?

Chapter 18: Change Is Constant—So Is Pain

Change. It is the only constant, they say. Sure, it sounds wise when printed on a motivational poster. But when change shows up unannounced—like a nosy neighbour, a sudden breakup, or a job loss—it feels less like wisdom and more like chaos.

And pain? Oh, pain is always the plus-one to change's party. Yet no one prepares us for how deeply it rearranges not just our plans but our sense of control. Instead of welcoming it as part of the process, most of us resist. The resistance creates frustration, anger, and those darker thoughts that quietly ask, Why is this happening?

Unchecked emotions like these lead to chaos far beyond our individual experience. They fuel prejudice, heated arguments, and divisions within families, workplaces, and communities. The lesson is simple yet often ignored: pain is not the villain. It is the guide.

I look at my peers and the loved ones around me. I hear about their childhoods—their mischief, adventures, and carefree joy—and I wonder: Wow, I was never a child. I can count the moments of happiness before the age of 23 on one hand. One is my father holding my hand, and the other is my mother blowing raspberries on my stomach—a sensation I can still feel today. Beyond that, the memories blur. Childhood for me wasn't adventurous, mischievous, or fun—it was intense, serious, and burdened. I have carried the weight of responsibility on my shoulders for as long as I can remember.

No wonder I gravitate towards children. They remind me of what I missed—the freedom to play, to laugh without reason, to exist without expectations. But perhaps that is the lesson: change is constant, and so is pain. The child I never was then can still live in the adult I am now. Pain leaves its mark, yes, but it also opens doors. Maybe the love I pour into children, into people, is my way of healing.

Then there is the pain (or thought) of losing someone you love feels like standing on the edge of a cliff. It leaves you breathless, the ground unsteadies beneath your feet. I have not been in that void myself, but even imagining it is enough to send a wave of panic through me. Thich Nhat Hanh once said that the people you love never really leave you—they are in the way you breathe, the way you live, and the way you love. It sounds comforting but let us be real—it does not make the ache disappear.

Grief is messy. People say, "Time will heal." Sure. Time does something, but it does not erase. It shifts. Grief never fades—it settles, it lingers, and it becomes part of who you are. Moving on? That's just another myth we're sold. You never move on; you find a way to live with it.

That's what grief is—it's love with nowhere to go. It never vanishes. It stays in your memories, in the way you laugh at their jokes even when no one else gets them, in the way you make choices because of what they taught you. Losing someone never means losing their love; it means learning how to carry it differently.

And no, it never stops hurting. But that pain? It's a reminder that they mattered, that their life meant something, and that their love lives on in you. That's the thing about loss—it breaks you, but it also builds you into something you never thought you could be.

If loss teaches you about grief, caregiving teaches you about exhaustion The storm of caregiving is beyond overwhelming. Nothing prepares you for it. When someone you in your life becomes critically ill, it's like your life gets hijacked. Suddenly, all their pain becomes your responsibility and you have to heal it. You're expected to show up—always. To give endlessly. To keep smiling even when you're barely holding it together. And you do it. Of course, you do it. Because you care. Because it feels like there's no other choice.

It's brutal. And the hardest part? It's not just the illness. It's the entitlement that sneaks in. Their frustration with life becomes frustration with you. The demands pile up. Sometimes fair, often not. And you? You keep giving, even when you've got nothing left.

Because guilt whispers in your ear: "If you stop, you're selfish. If you step back, you're the bad guy."

∞

But here's the truth no one tells you: caregiving isn't about bleeding yourself dry. It is critical for caregivers to shield themselves. Think of shields as a safety valve—allowing in only what you can handle, without completely shutting off from the world. Shields are not selfish. Shields are what keep you standing when everything else is pulling you down. They are not walls. They let you care without losing yourself. Without a shield, you give until there is nothing left, and then what? Shields are how you protect what matters without destroying yourself in the process. They're the only thing standing between you and breaking. You never need to burn yourself out to prove you care. And yes, that's hard to hear. Because we've been conditioned to believe that love, caring, kindness means sacrifice—no limits, no boundaries. But if you lose yourself completely, what good are you to anyone?

Caregiving strips you bare. It shows you who you really are—and not always in ways you're proud of.

It'll bring out your compassion and your rage. It'll break you and rebuild you, and not always neatly. There's no manual for this. You stumble, you screw up, you second-guess everything. And somehow, you keep going. Not perfectly, but with enough strength to face another day. That's not weakness. That's what being human looks like.

Thich Nhat Hanh taught that equanimity offers steadiness in these storms of life. The chaos may rage, but within the centre, calm can exist. This is not a passive calm but an active choice to face discomfort with clarity rather than fear. The practice of equanimity requires patience, and it reveals its rewards gradually. It is not about avoiding the storm— it is about standing firm within it.

There have been many times—and still are—when life threw unexpected change my way, and it felt relentless. I found myself in a job I loved and truly adored. It gave me financial stability and a clear path to grow. Yet, it ended abruptly—not because of a lack of performance but due to redundancy. The decision was cold and political, leaving me questioning not just the role but the system I had placed my trust in.

Years later, I found myself in another role where my refusal to be a yes man and my unwillingness to compromise wholesome values gradually built tension. In 2011, I made the choice to leave, once again questioning not just the role but the entire structure I had once believed in.

Then there was my divorce—a chapter I thought was permanent that suddenly closed. The path to divorce was not overnight but was triggered by my redundancy. Over the years, the relationship was bleeding to death, forcing me to let go, not just of a person but of a beautiful dream that no longer was in my reality. The truth is, I was the culprit. I had someone so precious, yet I forgot her.

It took me years to heal and to even begin considering a new relationship. But that journey came with its own betrayals and heartbreaks. One relationship ended with her cheating on me. Another felt threatened by my calmness, as though my stillness reflected something unsettling in herself. Then there was someone who accused me of cheating on her.

After years of healing, I finally found myself in a beautiful six-year relationship with someone I was going to get married to. It was a bond I had nurtured with care; one I believed was built on trust and mutual respect. And then, in the snap of a message, it ended. Gone. Just like that. The dark void returned, and with it came the familiar ache of loss.

And then there's the other kind of loss—the one that comes not from people, but from security itself. As if life wanted to add more weight, I faced the constant struggle of not earning enough to achieve financial stability. The pressure was crushing, each bill a reminder of how far I felt from solid ground. Every time I thought I had found a solution; it slipped through my fingers. Frustration, anger, and hopelessness were constant companions.

I resisted every one of these changes. I clung to the life I thought I was supposed to have, holding on tighter and tighter, as if sheer willpower could bend reality to my expectations. But the tighter I held on, the heavier it all became. Each step forward felt like dragging myself uphill with no summit in sight.

Then slowly, slowly, slowly, something shifted—not overnight, not magically, but gradually. Instead of fighting to control every detail, I began to focus only on what I could truly influence. I began to let go—not of action, but of the illusion of control. The pain did not vanish, but it shifted. It became less of an enemy and more of a teacher. It showed me resilience, clarity, and the strength to navigate what I thought I could not endure.

What I have learned is this: pain is part of the journey, yet it need not define it. When pain guides rather than derails, something shifts. Frustration fades. Fear loses its grip. Change, messy as it is, becomes a great teacher.

Look at the world around you. Seasons shift. Rivers reshape the land. Even mountains erode over time. Why, then, do we cling to the idea that life should remain still and predictable? Change is the nature of existence, and pain is the friction that creates transformation.

∞

EXPLORATION TIME
What can you do when pain and change feel overwhelming?

Acknowledge the pain without fighting it. Pain is never your enemy but a signal that transformation is taking place.

Shift your focus to what you can regulate. Release the need to control outcomes and instead focus on your responses and wholesome efforts. Allow yourself to grieve the old while welcoming the new. Healing means honouring what was while making space for what can be.

Seek the lesson, not just relief. Let pain reveal what needs to shift rather than rushing to numb it.

Embrace the discomfort as part of growth. True change often feels messy and uncertain—yet it is where growth truly happens.

When life throws its inevitable surprises—and it always will—pause. Breathe deeply, not to suppress the discomfort, but to acknowledge it fully. Feel the emotions rise and fall like waves, knowing they will eventually recede. Change is constant, and pain is often the friction that fuels growth.

Suffering, however, is often not a conscious choice. As the Buddha taught in the Four Noble Truths, suffering arises not only from attachment and clinging to expectations but also from deeper patterns of karma—the echoes of past actions, both personal and ancestral, that ripple through lifetimes.

Modern science mirrors this wisdom, acknowledging how unresolved trauma can be inherited across generations, embedding itself in the body and mind. True healing begins not with suppression but with the courage to break these cycles through awareness, compassion, and self-inquiry.

And in the middle of all this mess—never forget to laugh when you can. Even in chaos, life has a way of slipping in moments of unexpected joy.

Stand firm in the storm, not against it. That is where strength and peace are found.

REFLECTION QUESTIONS
How have you resisted change in the past, and what impact did it have on your growth?
What small step can you take today to release control and embrace transformation?
How can you begin to see pain as a teacher rather than an enemy?

Chapter 19: Growth Is Not a Straight Line

Let us set the record straight: I was never the typical "smart kid." Teachers looked at me and saw... well, not much. Some said I was stupid. Others whispered I had no brain, only a peanut up there. I was the student they politely described as "trying," or they'd say, "He'll come to nothing." And honestly, I was not great at studies. I admit it. I never cared enough to memorise equations or ace history exams. The system said grades were everything, and since I was not topping the charts, the world around me assumed my potential was microscopic.

What a joke. Growth has nothing to do with grades. It does not follow a syllabus, and it certainly never cares about your report card. Growth stumbles into your life uninvited, often disguised as heartbreak, redundancy, or betrayal. It is not the tidy ladder they sell us—it is a drunken zigzag, dirty and unpredictable. And yet, somehow, it always finds you.

Now, let me clarify. I am a strong promoter of education—education that is practical, insightful, and encourages openness, creativity, and innovation. Education that expands minds rather than labelling them. What I cannot stand is the kind of education that boxes you, restricts you, and makes you feel worthless just because you unable to fit a narrow definition of "smart." That kind of system failed me— and it fails so many others.

In my teens, my dream was to be an actor. I wanted to be on stage and the silver screen, stepping into characters, telling stories, captivating audiences. Hey, my drama teacher, Ms. Richards, even came home to convince my parents to send me to drama school. But life had other plans—or rather, my conservative, strict family had other plans. They were having none of that. It was their life plan for me, not mine. I ended up in IT—logical, predictable, and about as far removed from acting as you could imagine. Growth, I thought, would come from climbing the corporate IT ladder. Spoiler: life laughed at my plans.

Then came redundancy—a big, ugly full stop. It felt like failure, the end of the road. But here is the twist: it was not the end. It was a massive bend in the road. Redundancy pushed me towards speaking, training, coaching and authoring —things I had no idea I could do.

Encouragement from the likes of Craig Chapman and Stuart Beaumont planted seeds I did not even realise were growing. In 2004, then there was Tim Foster who told me, "You have a natural talent for developing others—never give that up." At the time, I thought he was just being polite. During the credit crunch in 2008, the wonderful Bryan Fuge said I was one of the greatest educators he had ever come across. Then there was Vernon Bryce who told me my unconventional style of not following the crowd was what made me brilliant. "Keep giving to the world this way," he said. I shrugged all it off then, but looking back, those words held weight. They stayed with me, even when I did not fully believe them myself.

Fast forward to now, and here I am—doing work I love. The credit has to go to all the people mentioned and especially my former wife. Till date she encourages me to do the best I can. Please not to romanticise this. Financial struggles have been constant companions. There are still days I question my path, days when I wonder, What's the point? And then, there are people like Mouna—one of my students. She often reminds me of how our work together transformed her life. It is not about ego—it is the quiet, humbling joy of knowing I made a difference.

Growth never waits for you to be ready. It barges in, uninvited, and demands your attention. My divorce? I did not ask for that. Betrayal, insecurity, and heartbreak? No thank you. But growth happened anyway. Pain forced me to confront myself, let go of what no longer served me, and rebuild from the ground up.

Growth loves to show up disguised as chaos. Betrayal from someone you trusted? Growth. Being accused of cheating when you never did? Growth. Realising your calmness unsettles others? Growth. None of it felt like progress in the moment. It felt like failure, loss, and doubt. But growth could not care less about your timeline. It finds you anyway—especially in the mess.

EXPLORATION TIME

How can you trust your growth, even when it feels messy and unclear?

Acknowledge the messy nature of growth. Progress often feels confusing, unclear, and even uncomfortable. Accept the chaos without judging it.

Release the idea of linear success. Growth is full of loops and setbacks. Allow yourself to evolve without needing a perfect timeline.

Revisit past challenges. Reflect on situations where you struggled but eventually grew stronger. Use those lessons to trust the process today.

Celebrate the small steps. Growth is not always about big leaps. Recognise the quiet victories along the way.

Embrace being a work in progress. Growth is not about reaching a final version of yourself—it is about evolving constantly with self-compassion.

Even in the everyday moments, growth creeps in. Saying no to a toxic workplace. Realising perfection is a trap that kills creativity. Each decision, each stumble, added another layer to the person I am today. Growth never follows a straight path, but every twist and turn matters.

And here is a truth no one talks about: growth rarely feels like growth when you are in it. It feels like walking through fog, unsure of where you are headed. It feels like falling, falling, and falling. But then clarity comes. A lesson learned. A new perspective gained. And suddenly, you realise how far you have come.

Society loves its neat success stories—the straight lines, the linear paths. Yes, they love the rag to riches stories to motivate others but tend to shun those who have not succeeded in their eyes even when they have done the best. Life never has and never will be a straightforward journey. It is a winding road filled with potholes, dead ends, unexpected views and cliffs you fall off. Thus, growth is not about reaching a destination; it is about embracing the chaos, the mess, and the absurdity of it all.

Growth has no rules or maps. Trust it, and you will find your way.

REFLECTION QUESTIONS
How have your past struggles shaped the person you are today?
What expectations about growth have held you back from fully embracing your journey?
How can you begin to see progress even when it feels invisible?

Chapter 20: You Are Being Done, Not Just Doing

We are called human beings, not human doings—but let's be real, most of us are living like human doo-doo. And yes, I mean it literally—poop, faeces, waste. Running around chaotically, driven by the wasteful idea that constant busyness equals worth. Hustle culture, that relentless cycle of grind and overwork, has sold us the idea that more effort equals more value. The result? Generations of people pushing themselves beyond their limits, sacrificing health, relationships, and meaning for goals they often cannot even define.

Hustle culture thrives on the idea that if you are not constantly doing, you are falling behind. You got to be working 28 hours a day, well on this planet we have 24 hours. Hustle culture convinces, demands and forces you that packed schedules and endless sacrifices mean progress. But are you truly moving forward, or is hustle culture moving you? Taoism teaches us a humbling truth: what we think we are controlling is often controlling us. Hustle culture makes you believe you are the one doing, but in reality, it is doing you. It keeps you trapped in a cycle of never feeling enough.

Even now, I find myself falling for it at times. Hustle culture surrounds us, shouting from every corner that overworking is a virtue. No matter how much awareness you have, there are moments when the grind pulls you back in. It is a constant battle to step away, reflect, and choose a different way of living.

This is the heartbreaking part: it is not only a personal struggle. The upcoming generations are being raised in this toxic culture of hustle. They are being taught that their worth lies in constant busyness. It is devastating to watch how deeply this mindset is damaging people. Working hard is important. Working smart is essential. Exploring passions is enriching. But hustling? That is a different story entirely.

Let's talk about the word itself. The dictionary defines "hustle" as: to push roughly, to force, or to move hurriedly in a specified direction. None of this sounds wholesome, does it? Hustle, in its essence, is about force—forcing outcomes, forcing progress, forcing yourself beyond what is sustainable. And while a push can occasionally be helpful, living in a constant state of hustle is damaging for everyone involved.

Burnout is more than exhaustion. It happens when you lose sight of why you are working in the first place. It happens when you are so busy doing that you forget how to simply be. And the impact extends far beyond the individual. Overworking isolates us. It creates disconnection from relationships, empathy, and the joys that make life meaningful.

Then there is the damaging idea of "Fake it till you make it." It tells you to pretend—to act confident, to appear like you have it all figured out, to cover up cracks with a smile. But faking does not solve anything. It is exhausting and unsustainable. You cannot fake your way through growth, pain, or doubt. You must face it.

Instead of faking it give a go at "Face it. Faith it. Make it." Facing it means owning your reality—the good, the bad, and the chaotic. Faithing, it means trusting that even without clarity, you are on the right path. Making it happens when you stop pretending and align with what truly matters. "Fake it till you make it" is about fooling yourself and others, but "face it, faith it, and make it" is about being honest with yourself. As my guardian angels always reminds me, you can lie to the world, but when you lie to yourself, then you are truly doomed.

Taoism provides another antidote through the concept of Wu Wei, or effortless action. It teaches us to flow with life instead of forcing outcomes. Wu Wei never suggests laziness or inaction. It means aligning your efforts with the natural flow, working with life rather than fighting against it. Hustle culture demands constant motion, constant grinding. Taoism asks, Why? Why push? And who decided this was worth chasing? Hustle culture profits from your exhaustion, but Wu Wei reminds us that clarity and alignment bring the best outcomes.

When I began questioning hustle culture, my perspective shifted. Success is not a title, a bank balance, or a destination. Success is the process of becoming—not just doing but being. Slowing down is not failure. Rest is not laziness. Both are necessary to reconnect with what truly matters.

EXPLORATION TIME
What can you do to break free from the grip of hustle culture?

Acknowledge the patterns driving your busyness. Reflect on whether your current pace is genuinely aligned with your values or simply a conditioned response to external pressure.

Experiment with intentional pauses. Take small moments throughout the day to step back— whether it is a deep breath, a mindful break, or a conscious check-in with yourself.

Redefine success on your own terms. Write down what true success looks like for you—beyond titles, income, or productivity—and let it guide your decisions.

Notice where you are forcing outcomes. Identify situations where you are pushing harder than necessary and explore if releasing control could allow more clarity and ease.

Commit to one practice of effortless alignment. Whether it is a daily reflection, saying no to unnecessary tasks, or prioritising rest, choose one action to create balance this week.

The hustle will never give permission to pause or tell you that you are enough. But Taoism quietly reminds you: you already are. There is no need to force, grind, or unnecessarily sacrifice yourself to prove worthiness. True alignment happens when you stop hustling and start flowing.

So, the next time hustle culture pulls you in, pause. Ask yourself: Am I doing this, or is this being done to me? Remember, there is nothing empowering and encouraging about being done.

You are a human being, not a human doo-doo.
Rest, reflect, and rejuvenate —because being is
where the real magic happens.

REFLECTION QUESTIONS
How has hustle culture shaped the way you
measure your worth?
Where in your life do you feel like you are being
"done" rather than consciously choosing?
What would it feel like to work in alignment with
your values instead of constantly pushing?

Chapter 21: Do Your Thing, Release the Outcome

The world loves to measure success by results. Did you win the competition? Did your plan succeed? Did you meet your goal? We live in a society that glorifies outcomes. Yet for all our obsession with results, they remain stubbornly out of reach. And that is the paradox—by fixating on outcomes, we lose the joy and focus that come from fully engaging in the act itself.

Look at how a country is measured by GDP year after year, as if economic growth alone defines its success. Throughout life, we are measured by the pressure of grades, reduced to exam scores that supposedly determine our worth. People judge us by what we drive, the postcode we live in, and the size of our bank accounts. And then, as if to sprinkle hypocrisy on top, we are served the pathetic lecture of honesty, integrity, and trust. Yet when someone dares to live by these values, the world scoffs. "You are unreal, too idealistic," they say. "This is the real world—ruthless, cutthroat. Those soft values never matter and will never matter."

This relentless focus on results creates a toxic cycle where self-worth becomes entangled with external validation. But what if true value lies not in results but in the care and presence we bring to our actions?

The Bhagavad Gita teaches us, "You have the right to perform your actions, but not the right to their results." In other words, focus on doing your thing. Give it your best but release any attachment to how it turns out. This practice, known as Karma Yoga, encourages us to act with full intention and effort, while letting go of the outcome. It is a philosophy that has guided millions toward clarity and peace.

Taoism reinforces this with its principle of Wu Wei, or effortless action. Imagine a tree bending in the wind. It does not resist; it flows with the force. A Taoist story tells of a farmer whose horse runs away. His neighbours say, "Such bad luck." The farmer simply responds, "Maybe." The next day, the horse returns with several wild horses. "Such good luck," say the neighbours. Again, the farmer replies, "Maybe." The point is clear: outcomes are not always what they seem. Taoism teaches us to release judgment, trust the flow, and act without grasping.

Sikhism offers a powerful perspective on this as well. The practice of seva, or selfless service, reminds us to contribute to the world without ego or expectation. Sikhs believe that true service comes from the heart, not from a desire for reward. This is why langar—the communal kitchen—is such a sacred practice. Feeding others, regardless of status, is an act of devotion performed purely for its own sake.

Confucianism, meanwhile, emphasises virtue over recognition. Confucius said, "The superior man is concerned with the root; when the root is established, the way is born." This root is virtue—doing what is right because it is right, not because it earns approval or reward. Confucian wisdom calls us to focus on the essence of our actions, not the applause they may or may not bring.

All of this sounds profound—and it is. But let's admit something: it can also be incredibly frustrating. How do you actually apply these teachings to daily life? How do you avoid attachment to outcomes in a world that constantly measures you by them? How do you "trust the flow" when bills are due, deadlines loom, and uncertainty feels overwhelming?

It starts with shifting focus to the effort itself. Instead of asking, Did I succeed? ask, Did I give my best? Success becomes less about the result and more about the care you bring to the act. An artist might focus on the joy of painting, not the potential of selling the work. A professional might take pride in doing their job well, regardless of external recognition.

Release the endless what-ifs. Replace "What if it doesn't work?" with "What can I give care and attention to right now?" Outcomes are unpredictable, but your actions in the present are fully within your reach. This mind flow brings clarity, even in moments of uncertainty.

There is also power in celebrating the process. Whether it is cooking a meal, writing a report, or building a relationship, meaning often lies in the act itself. The Stoic principle of Amor Fati, or "love of fate," offers a profound perspective. It challenges us to embrace all outcomes—good or bad—as part of our path. Instead of resisting what happens, learn to accept it as an opportunity for growth.

And perhaps most importantly, reflect. At the end of each day, ask yourself: Did I act with intention? Did I bring care and attention to the process? Did I stay present? These questions anchor us in the moment and help us let go of results we cannot determine.

Modern psychology supports this shift in focus. Studies on intrinsic motivation show that people are happier and more fulfilled when they act out of alignment with their values, rather than chasing external rewards. Flow states, as described by Mihaly Csikszentmihalyi, occur when we lose ourselves in the process of what we are doing, with little concern for results. The less we obsess over outcomes, the more likely we are to find joy, clarity, and even success.

EXPLORATION TIME
What can you do to release attachment to outcomes and stay focused on meaningful action?

Identify what you can regulate. Focus your energy on the process—your effort, attention, and mind flow—instead of obsessing over results.

Clarify your intentions. Ask yourself, "Am I acting from a place of care and integrity, or am I driven by external validation?"

Practice presence in small actions. Bring full awareness to daily activities—whether it is a conversation, a task, or a creative project.

Reflect on past experiences. Notice moments where releasing attachment led to unexpected positive outcomes and growth.

Commit to a daily check-in. At the end of each day, ask yourself: "Did I give my best effort today, regardless of the outcome?"

So, what does this look like in practice? It looks like showing up fully for what matters. It looks like putting care into the present moment, not the distant outcome. It looks like trusting that the act itself is enough. Do your thing. Paint the masterpiece. Write the book. Cook the meal. Serve others. And let the outcome unfold as it may.

This is not about giving up ambition or goals. It does not mean you stop striving—it means you shift from being obsessed with results to being committed to the process. Success often follows those who are deeply engaged in their work, not those who anxiously chase it. It means reorienting your energy toward what you can give care and attention to: your effort, your presence, and your integrity. It is about aligning.

Taoism asks us to flow. Sikhism reminds us to serve. Confucianism calls us to virtue. The Bhagavad Gita guides us to act with intention, while Stoicism challenges us to embrace fate. Together, they offer a liberating truth: do what aligns with your wholesome values and let go of what you cannot determine.

Do the wholesome thing, no matter what the outcome—because the act itself is where life's truth lies.

REFLECTION QUESTIONS
What areas of your life have been controlled by attachment to results?
How would your experience shift if you focused on the process rather than the outcome?
What actions can you take today with full intention, regardless of the results?

Chapter 22: The Subconscious: What We Carry Without Knowing

Have you ever reacted to something and thought, "Where did that come from?" Or caught yourself saying something and wondered, "Was that even me?" Welcome to the subconscious—your mind's quiet operator working behind the scenes while you convince yourself you're in control. It works silently, shaping how you think, act, and feel based on beliefs, patterns, and habits absorbed long before you became aware of them. And here's the real kicker—most of what's in there never originated from you.

The subconscious is like an attic filled with boxes you've never unpacked. Some of those boxes belong to you—childhood memories, fears, desires—but many are from others. Generational trauma, cultural programming, and societal expectations are stacked high, shaping the labyrinth you walk through every day without even realising it. Yet, instead of questioning this complexity, motivational quick fixes and oversimplified solutions are often thrown at us like confetti at a party we didn't even want to attend.

Take the famous phrase, "What you think, you become." It is often falsely attributed to Buddha, but let's be blunt—this is a distorted half-truth dressed up as wisdom. Buddha never taught some shallow version of positive thinking. His teachings went far deeper, rooted in karmic seeds—the repeated habits, thoughts, and intentions that influence reality over lifetimes. But twisting this complex truth into a motivational soundbite has created toxic positivity at its worst.

This reductionist nonsense makes people believe that every struggle, trauma, and failure is their fault for "thinking wrong." It shames those already in pain, telling them their suffering is a mindset problem instead of acknowledging the weight of subconscious conditioning, generational wounds, and societal oppression. It is not enlightenment. It is emotional gaslighting, and it messes people up.

You cannot just "think" your way out of deep-seated trauma, systemic struggles, or years of unexamined beliefs. True growth demands facing the uncomfortable shadows within, not wallpapering over pain with pretty words.

Or consider the broken record of "Reprogram your mind, and you reprogram your life." The subconscious is not a gadget that can be rebooted in a few seconds or minutes. It is a messy attic filled with forgotten boxes and misplaced memories. Real transformation requires understanding what's inside—opening those boxes, deciding what to keep, and finding the courage to let go of what no longer serves you.

And then there's the classic—brace yourself— "Change your thoughts, and you change your world." On the surface, it feels empowering, but the subconscious operates far deeper than surface-level thoughts. It is a maze of inherited beliefs, buried emotions, and unresolved fears. Changing it requires patience, curiosity, and a willingness to sit with the uncomfortable truths about what you carry.

The most challenging part? Much of what shapes your subconscious is not yours to begin with. Generational trauma, societal norms, and cultural expectations have left their marks, influencing how you view success, relationships, and self-worth. It's like wandering through a labyrinth designed by others, trying to navigate paths you never chose.

This is where practices like Morrnah Simeona's version of Ho'oponopono offer profound help. Morrnah taught that memories—personal and inherited—act as energetic imprints influencing your present. The practice of Ho'oponopono allows space for releasing, cleansing, healing, and transmuting. It is not aimed at controlling the subconscious; it appeals to Divinity itself. By taking responsibility—not as blame, but as an opportunity for healing—you create room to release what weighs you down.

EXPLORATION TIME

What can you do to begin working with your subconscious mind instead of being ruled by it?

Observe your emotional triggers. The next time you react strongly to a situation, pause. Ask yourself, "What belief or past experience is being triggered here?"

Unpack your mental attic. Write down beliefs you have about success, love, and self-worth. Reflect on where they originated—are they truly yours?

Practice self-inquiry. Give a go at journaling with prompts like, "Whose voice am I hearing when I self-criticise?" or "What assumptions do I carry that limit me?"

Release old patterns with compassion. If a belief no longer serves you, acknowledge it. Thank it for helping to protect you and gently choose a healthier perspective.

Integrate awareness into daily life. Use mindfulness practices like Vipassana meditation to become more aware of thought patterns without reacting to them.

The subconscious is not something to conquer. It is not an opponent to defeat but a labyrinth to explore. Begin by observing your patterns with curiosity. What triggers you? What holds you back? Ask yourself, Whose voice is this? The critic in your head—does it belong to you, or is it an echo from parents, teachers, or society?

The subconscious is not your enemy; it is a part of you that has been doing its best to protect you, even if its methods no longer work. By understanding it, you begin working with it rather than against it. The subconscious is a labyrinth we navigate unknowingly, shaped by experiences, beliefs, deep seated traumas and inherited generational patterns.

Facing the subconscious mind with honesty may never bring instant peace, yet each step through its winding paths reveals deeper understanding and the freedom to move forward with intention.

REFLECTION QUESTIONS
What beliefs and patterns have you inherited that no longer serve you?
How can you begin recognising the subconscious patterns influencing your decisions?
What would shifting from reacting to observing your subconscious patterns look like in your life?

Chapter 23: Karma Is Going To Get You

Karma. The word has been turned into a cheap punchline. "Karma's coming for them," people say, as if karma is a cosmic hitman, patiently waiting to avenge their petty grievances. Social media loves to slap it on memes as if adding a Sanskrit word to a cat picture suddenly gives them depth. Let's cut through the nonsense: karma is real, but it does not work the way you think it does.

Karma is not your personal cosmic cheerleader. It remembers everything—every choice, every ripple, no matter how small or big. It is relentless, impartial, and deeply personal. Sometimes, it will ambush you when you least expect it, striking from places you never anticipated. Other times, it gives you subtle signs— nudges, whispers, patterns echoing in your life. And occasionally, it comes from every direction, all at once, as if the universe decided it was finally time for you to face your actions.

In Sanskrit, karma simply means "action." Every thought, word, and deed send ripples into the world—ripples that interact, amplify, and return in ways you can neither predict nor control. There's no fairness to it, no moral ledger balancing the scales. Karma has no care if you're the kindest soul on Earth or an unapologetic narcissist. It operates on one deep principle: cause and effect.

Cause and effect are simple: everything you do creates a ripple. Think of it like dropping a pebble into water—your action (the cause) sends out waves (the effect). These waves never disappear; they keep moving, touching everything in their path. Sometimes they come back to you quickly, like throwing a ball against a wall. Other times, they travel far, mix with other waves, and return much later, altered but still connected to you. Every choice you make—big or small—sets something in motion. Those ripples shape the world around you and the reality you experience.

Yes, it's similar to the butterfly effect, but with a more personal twist. The butterfly effect suggests that small actions—like the flap of a butterfly's wings—can set off a chain reaction leading to massive outcomes far away, like a storm on the other side of the world.

Karma, or cause and effect, works in a similar way, but the ripples are tied to your feelings, actions, thoughts, and intentions. The choices you make may feel insignificant—a kind word, a careless insult—but they create waves that travel outward, affecting people and situations you may never see. Over time, those waves mix with others, amplifying or shifting their energy, until they eventually return to you in unexpected ways.

So yes, karma and the butterfly effect share the idea that small actions can lead to big consequences—but karma adds the layer of personal responsibility. Your actions change the environment and they shape the life you live.

Let me say it plainly—karma isn't mystical. It's biological. Neuroscience has shown that repeated actions and habits carve grooves into your brain, shaping the way you think and act. Kindness rewires you for connection, while deceit hardwires stress and isolation. Behavioural psychology proves it too: your choices ripple through social networks, affecting people you've never even met. A simple act of generosity might inspire someone continents away. But here's the kicker: karma doesn't stop there. It's not just about the external ripples; it's about the internal ones. Every time you lie, cheat, or act with malice, you erode a part of yourself. The damage isn't always visible, but it's there.

Yet, karma has been hijacked by the self-help industry. Karma is not your spiritual soundbite or a quick hack to tidy up your life. Toss out the fluff about "manifesting reality" or "attracting what you deserve." Karma never waits for hashtags or sings of every action, spinning a web so intricate no mind can fully predict its design. It flows silently, threading your choices into a reality you'll eventually have to face, whether you like it or not.

Let's get raw. Karma never makes sense. Sometimes, it feels like the universe skipped a step. Good people suffer. Horrible people thrive. It's infuriating. And it's real. The ripples you send out interact with countless others, creating waves you have no control over. Your actions are just one thread in a vast, tangled web of cause and effect. Karma is the ocean; you're just a swimmer. You cannot control the tides; you ride them. The ancient traditions understood this far better than modern life coaches ever will.

Just as individuals carry karma, so do families, communities, and even entire nations. Generational karma passes through actions, choices, and unspoken lessons. Breaking these cycles requires awareness—not just of what you do, but of the patterns you've inherited.

EXPLORATION TIME
What can you do to live with greater awareness of your karma?

Acknowledge your ripples. Pay attention to how your actions and words influence those around you. Notice the subtle impact you create, both positive and negative.

Clarify your intentions. Before speaking or acting, ask yourself: Is this coming from a place of care, fear, or ego?

Own your patterns. Reflect on recurring life experiences. Are they results of repeated behaviours or unresolved patterns?

Practice mindful presence. Focus on aligning your current actions with integrity, regardless of past mistakes.

Release the need for cosmic justice. Stop expecting karma to deliver revenge or rewards—focus instead on living from values, not outcomes.

But here's where it gets tricky. You'll never fully see karma in action. Some ripples take lifetimes to return. Others hit you square in the face before you've had time to process what you did. And sometimes, karma skips you entirely, landing on your children or grandchildren instead. It asks for no permission, and it certainly has no care for your schedule. Karma is relentless, impartial, and deeply personal. It's not here to fix your life or punish your enemies. It's simply the energy you create coming back to greet you.

Karma is not here to play by your rules. It has no interest in whether you believe you have suffered enough or whether someone else deserves a taste of their own medicine. You might pour everything into doing good and still wonder why life keeps throwing chaos at you. Meanwhile, the one who caused you pain seems to walk free, untouched. That is the nature of karma—it is not a neat equation or a system you can control. It moves as it pleases, following ripples you may never see. The only certainty is this: what you give to the world—good or bad—will return in some way. Maybe not to you, maybe not in this lifetime, but it will return. Your only job is to keep moving forward, knowing the energy you create matters, even if you never see the results.

Do what is wise because it challenges you to question, grow, and keep moving forward, even when life feels unfair.

REFLECTION QUESTIONS:

What patterns from your past continue to shape your present?

How can you create positive ripples in your current relationships and actions?

In what ways can you release attachment to expecting results from your actions?

Part IV: Through Chaos, We Found Ourselves

Part III explored how work, growth, and hustle shape the way we connect with the world and strive for external success. But what happens when external systems fail to sustain us? When chaos takes over, and the path forward is uncertain, what keeps us steady? What allows us to face the storm without losing ourselves in its fury?

Part IV is a journey into the principles that anchor us amidst life's turbulence. It is not about striving harder or achieving more; it is about cultivating the timeless qualities that enable us to navigate chaos with grace and emerge stronger. Courage, clarity, conviction, compassion, equanimity, and mind flow—these are not lofty ideals. They are the lifelines that pull make us move forward when life unravels, and the compass that guides us back to ourselves.

Courage is not the absence of fear but the quiet resolve to face it. Clarity is not having all the answers but seeing through the noise to recognise what truly matters. Conviction is not stubbornness but standing firm in our truth with humility. Compassion is not weakness but the greatest strength we can offer ourselves and others. Equanimity is not detachment but the art of remaining steady in the face of life's storms. And mind-flow is not rigidity but the power to move like water, adapting and flowing without losing our essence.

This section bridges the external and internal, taking us from the hustle of doing to the art of being. It is an invitation to reflect deeply on the essence of resilience, presence, and authenticity. These are not traits we master overnight but practices we return to, again and again, shaping how we endure, how we grow, and how we find meaning even in the most chaotic moments.

Through chaos, we do not merely survive—we find ourselves. We uncover the strength we did not know we had, the clarity that cuts through confusion, and the compassion that holds us steady. These principles are not here to fix us; they are here to remind us of what has always been within us.

Welcome to Part IV: Through Chaos, We Found Ourselves.

Chapter 24. Courage: It's Not What You Think

On 10 January 2021, I was staring death in the face. COVID had hijacked my lungs, turned my oxygen levels into a cruel joke, and pneumonia decided to make itself at home. Rent free tenant, a squatter. Breathing—something so ordinary I had never even thought about—was suddenly the hardest thing I had ever done. Each breath felt like dragging air through a brick wall, and every exhale carried the weight of uncertainty. Death was not a distant idea; it was right there, leaning over me, daring me to hold on. A reminder that death is only a breath away.

The hospital was a battlefield. The machines beeped relentlessly, the lights burned into me deeply, and the nurses—bless them—kept moving with a kind of calm I will never understand. I, on the other hand, was falling apart in every possible way. My body refused to cooperate, my mind spiralled, and my wholesome emotions hung by a thread. The only thing I could do was trust. Trust the doctors. Trust the nurses. Trust this failing and exhausted body to keep going.

And then there was the advice. Oh, the relentless messages. "Fight this! You have got to beat it! Show it who is boss!" Really? I could not even lift my head off the pillow, let alone take on a global pandemic. Let me tell you the truth—I never fought. I never "crushed it." I never summoned some warrior spirit from within. I did the one thing that made sense: I let go. I stopped attempting to control the uncontrollable. I stopped resisting what was happening. I surrendered—not as a sign of defeat but as an act of trust. I told life, "Do what you have to do. I will be here."

Surrender carries a bad reputation. People assume it means giving up. It is the opposite. It is facing the chaos head-on and saying, "I need to be here. The best I can." Surrender is courage in its purest form— not the loud, chest-thumping kind, but the quiet, unshakable kind that keeps you breathing when it feels impossible.

Fear? Oh, it was there. It sat with me, whispering all the things I wished I could ignore: "This is it. You are not going to make it." But instead of shoving it away, I let it stay.

Courage is not the absence of fear—it is making room for it. Fear is not the enemy. It is part of the journey. Courage does not kick fear out of the room. It sits down next to it and says, "Alright, you are here, but you are not running the show."

And let me tell you, courage is not pretty. Forget the motivational posters and the movie speeches. Real courage is raw. It is awkward. It is crying silently and sometimes out aloud at 2 a.m. because you are terrified yet still showing up for the next breath. Courage is trusting when there are no guarantees. It is letting go of control when every instinct demands you hold on tighter.

Rumi had it right in The Guest House. He said to welcome every emotion—joy, sorrow, fear—like a visitor. My visitors? Disease, anxiety, fear, anger, frustration, worry, depression, and much more barged in uninvited. Despair unpacked its bags, and uncertainty decided to linger indefinitely. The surprise? When you let them in, they lose their grip on you. Courage is not about slamming the door on fear;

it is about opening it wide and saying, "Come in. Stay as long as you need. I am still here."

In those moments, courage feels like nothing. There are no medals, no applause, no triumphant music. This is not some melodramatic drama or movie. It is just you, holding on to the smallest thread of hope but, more importantly, trust. When you look back, you realise courage was there all along, quietly keeping you alive and kicking.

EXPLORATION TIME
What can you do to cultivate genuine courage, even in moments of fear?

Acknowledge your fear. Never suppress it. Allow yourself to feel it fully, understanding it is not a weakness but a natural response to the unknown.

Redefine courage. Remind yourself that courage is not about fighting or conquering—it is about staying present and trusting the process, even when the outcome remains uncertain.

Breathe through discomfort. Practise conscious breathing when fear arises. Anchor yourself in the rhythm of your breath to stay grounded in the moment.

Release the need for control. Trust that you can only influence the present moment. Let go of the need to control outcomes you cannot predict.

Speak your truth. Share your fears with someone you trust. Verbalising vulnerability often reduces its power and creates space for deeper support.

Think about the farmer staring at barren fields during yet another season of drought. The soil is cracked, debts pile up, and every seed feels like a gamble. They have no certainty. They have no guarantees. They wake up before dawn, planting in land that has betrayed them before, because stopping is not an option. That is courage.

It is not poetic or noble. It is brutal. It is raw. It is putting one foot in front of the other when everything inside you screams to stop. It is showing up when the odds are stacked, when there is no applause, no glory. It is not pretty—it is survival with trembling hands, a defiant whisper: "I will not quit."

So, let me ask you: Are you ready to stop chasing the idea of courage and start living the reality of it? Because at its core, courage is not about being fearless or perfect—it is about standing firm, not rigid, trembling hands and all, and saying, "I am still here."

Courage embraces chaos and turns it into the power to persist, strive and thrive.

REFLECTION QUESTIONS:
When was the last time you faced fear and showed courage in small but significant ways?
How do you respond when life feels uncontrollable, and what could surrender look like for you?
What fear are you holding onto today, and how might you release its grip by simply allowing it to exist?

Chapter 25. Clarity: Seeing Through the Fog

The ICU. Beeping machines. Oxygen masks. A bed that feels more like both a physical restraint and an emotional trap, making healing feel distant rather than comforting.

It was not a place for profound moments or cinematic revelations. It was survival, plain and simple—a relentless fight to stay alive. And yet, even in the middle of that chaos, something unexpected stirred. A moment of clarity—raw, unsettling, and absolutely necessary.

Let me paint the picture for you. I was lying there, body barely cooperating, machines keeping me alive, and my mind—oh, it was replaying every regret, every wasted moment, every distraction I had ever let run my life on a relentless loop. And then, out of nowhere, a thought cut through the noise: "You are alive. That is enough."

Clarity is not this polished, media clickbait moment people use to scream, "Look at me! I am so strong! Give me likes and comments! Now let me be your guru and pretend I am not a guru while charging you a mere million dollars for the wisdom." Yes, we all fall for it—some more than others.

But real clarity? It never comes wrapped in wisdom or tied up with a neat little bow. Clarity is a slap across the face. It is that uncomfortable mirror forcing you to look at what you have been running from. In that ICU bed, clarity was not some grand revelation. It was the menacing truth: I had been wasting so much time chasing things that did not matter. And now? Now, all that mattered was the next breath.

Life loves throwing fog at us, a master illusionist. Expectations, doubts, the endless cycle of "what ifs"— they all swirl around, making it hard to see what is in front of us. And let us be real—most of the time, we are just fumbling through it, pretending we have it together. Clarity is not about finding a way out of the fog. It is about realising that you need not see everything clearly to keep moving.

And here is the truth no one tells you: clarity is not comfortable. It is not about feeling good. It is about ripping off the blinders and seeing things for what they really are. Clarity never waits for the perfect moment. It shows up when your world is falling apart, taps you on the shoulder, and says, "Ready to deal with this yet?"

EXPLORATION TIME
What can you do to cultivate clarity when life feels clouded?

Pause and create stillness. Clarity cannot emerge in constant noise. Create intentional moments of silence—whether through meditation, quiet reflection, or even a simple walk in nature.

Acknowledge the fog. Instead of fighting confusion, accept it as part of the process. Recognise that clarity often arises after we stop resisting the discomfort.

Ask better questions. Shift from "Why is this happening to me?" to "What am I being shown

here?" Thoughtful questions spark reflection and insight.

Let go of needing all the answers. Clarity often reveals just the next step, not the entire path. Trust that the next piece will appear when needed.

Reflect on past moments of clarity. Remember times when things eventually made sense. Trust that if it happened before, it would happen again.

The thing about clarity is it never sticks around forever. It is fleeting, like a break in the storm. You get a glimpse of the path ahead, and then the fog rolls back in. That is just how it works. Clarity is not some permanent state of enlightenment. It is a moment, a flicker, just enough light to take the next step. And that is all you need.

Think about the garbage collector. They show up, empty your bins, and disappear. Most of us never know their name, their face, or their story, but for that moment, they bring clarity to the chaos of your waste. Without them, your life would pile up with things you cannot handle. Clarity works the same way. It arrives, does its job, and then it is gone. You will not always understand it, and you will not always see it coming, but it clears enough of the mess to show you the next move. The rest is up to you to figure out.

Clarity is not about making the fog disappear. It is about learning to walk through it, bruised and unsure, and still finding the courage to take the next step. One imperfect, tricky step at a time.

REFLECTION QUESTIONS
When was the last time you experienced a moment of clarity during a difficult situation?
How do you respond when life feels unclear? Do you seek control, or can you allow space for clarity to emerge?
What small action can you take today to create more space for clarity in your life?

Chapter 26. Conviction: Knowing Without Arrogance

Let me take you back to that ICU bed. Machines were humming, oxygen was being forced into my lungs, and every breath felt like a negotiation with life itself. The uncertainty was unbearable. My body had betrayed me, and my mind was not far behind. But amidst the madness, something unexpected began to emerge—a quiet, unshakable knowing: I was going to get through this. Whether that meant living through it or facing death with grace, there was courage and clarity in that moment—an acceptance, not attachment.

This was not blind optimism or some feel-good mantra. It was conviction. And let me be clear—it was not the kind of arrogant conviction that says, "I know better than anyone else." No, this was different. It was rooted in something deeper, something unexplainable, a quiet strength that did not demand to be seen but was undeniably present. It was not about certainty; it was about trust. Trust in the doctors and nurses, trust in the process, trust in my body to stay strong even when it felt like it was giving up. Trust that I could face whatever came next, not with defiance but with courage.

Conviction is not about being loud or forceful. It is not about shouting your truth from the rooftops or bulldozing others with your beliefs. True conviction is quiet. It is steady. It is the ability to stand firm in what you know, without needing to prove it to anyone else. It is not about arrogance; it is about alignment, a resonance between your core values and your actions.

The difference between conviction and belief is stark. Do you know you are breathing? Or do you simply believe you are? Knowing is unshaken, grounded in faith and trust—a certainty that needs no external validation. Belief, however, carries an undertone of doubt, a veil of "what if." Belief often leads to forcing yourself to "fake it till you make it."

Knowing, on the other hand, invites you to "face it, faith it, and you will make it." Knowing builds a foundation of strength, adaptability, and resilience. It transforms doubt and hope into trust and hesitation into action. It is the voice that says, "I may not have all the answers, but I will keep going."

Conviction flows naturally as it is rooted in knowing. It does not waver, and it does not shout. It inspires, not through force, but through quiet confidence. Conviction turns ideas into actions and actions into results. It is not arrogance; it is equanimity. It gives you the strength to carry on, even when the path is unclear. When you know, you hope no longer—you simply trust and become.

The problem with conviction is that it is often mistaken for stubbornness. People think conviction means never backing down, never changing your mind. But real conviction is flexible. It knows when to stand firm and when to adapt. It is not about clinging to your beliefs; it is about living them and being versatile with them, evolving without compromising your integrity.

EXPLORATION TIME
What can you do to cultivate conviction in your life?

Identify the truths you know deeply. Reflect on what you feel unshakably certain about—beyond societal expectations or external influences. These truths may not be the loudest, but they resonate the deepest.

Embrace discomfort without retreat. Let conviction guide you through challenges rather than avoiding them. Clarity often arises not from ease but from enduring the storm.

Release the need for external validation. Conviction never demands applause. It is about internal alignment, the quiet strength that needs no permission to exist.

Stay open to growth. True conviction allows room for learning and adaptation while standing firm on core values. Flexibility does not weaken conviction—it refines it.

Build resilience through consistent actions. Each small, honest step you take strengthens your inner trust and quiet confidence. Conviction grows stronger with practice, not performance.

∞

In that ICU, my conviction was simple: I would face whatever came next, breath by breath. It was not grand or heroic. It was yuck and imperfect, but it was real. Conviction is not about certainty; it is about resilience. It is about trusting yourself, even when everything around you feels unstable.

Conviction is not a declaration shouted to the world. It is the quiet, steady pulse that reminds you of who you are and what you stand for. It grows stronger when tested, not weaker. Conviction keeps you moving forward, even when clarity wavers.

Conviction stands not for validation but for the quiet courage to move forward, steady and aligned with what truly matters—while giving clarity the strength to rise.

REFLECTION QUESTIONS:
What truths do you feel most certain about in your life?

∞

How do you distinguish between conviction and stubbornness in your decisions?
When was the last time you acted with quiet conviction, even when no one else understood your choice?

Chapter 27. Compassion: The Toughest Gift You Can Give

Compassion is a word often spoken yet rarely understood in its full depth. I thought I knew its meaning, but the ICU stripped me of all control and dignity, teaching me otherwise. This was not a time for dramatic revelations. It was survival—painful and relentless. Yet, in that darkness, compassion emerged. It did not whisper; it just reached for me gently.

But here is the truth: it was not my compassion. It was theirs. The nurse who adjusted my oxygen mask with a tenderness I will never forget. The doctor who, in the midst of saving lives, took a moment to meet my eyes and remind me I was still human. These were not acts of pity or duty. They were acts of courage. Because real compassion demands vulnerability, energy, and care without expectation.

In that room, surrounded by machines humming in clinical rhythm, I realised that compassion is not about fixing. It is about presence. It is standing beside someone in their most fragile moments, even when it forces you to confront discomfort. Compassion is both gentle and unyielding—not aggressive, not arrogant, but quietly powerful.

Let us be clear: compassion is difficult. It does not come with guarantees. It often feels thankless, uncomfortable, even harrowing. And yet, that is what makes it the hardest gift you can give. Compassion requires showing up fully, saying, "I see your pain, and I am here."

Now, let us shift focus. Compassion for others can be profound—but compassion for yourself? That is the harder battle. Lying in that hospital bed, weak and broken, my instinct was self-blame. Every poor choice, every ignored warning, every reckless decision played on repeat in my mind. Compassion for myself was the last thing I felt capable of.

Yet, in those moments, courage, clarity and conviction emerged. Compassion is not about excusing. It is about acknowledging. It is facing your flaws and saying, "Yes, you have made mistakes. And you are still worthy of care." Self-compassion is not indulgence. It is a lifeline. The quiet voice that interrupts self-criticism and whispers, "You are still human. And that is enough."

EXPLORATION TIME
How can you deepen true compassion in your life?

Acknowledge pain without forcing to fix it. Compassion is not about finding solutions. It is about presence—being there without the need to offer advice.

Embrace self-compassion. When self-criticism rises, pause and extend to yourself the same kindness you would offer a friend.

Listen fully. Compassion expands when we listen to understand, not just to respond. Let others and yourself feel truly heard.

Give without attachment. Real compassion is not transactional. Offer help where you can, even if it goes unnoticed.

Respect your own limits. Compassion is not self-sacrifice. It is showing up from a place of strength, not depletion.

Compassion demands bravery. It asks you to show up, even when it feels uncomfortable, even when you have no answers. Sometimes, it leads you to healing slowly, step by step. Other times, it transforms everything in an instant. The gift of compassion is its ability to share the weight of pain, making it bearable and building deeper connections.

Reflecting on my journey, I realise that compassion has been a central theme in my life and work, especially highlighted in my talks on the TED platform.

In "The Miracle of Compassion," I explore how we with compassion can nurture relationships, build trust, and act with mindfulness. These qualities lead to increased engagement, inspiring a more peaceful, abundant, and progressive life.

In "An Appointment With Life: Taking Refuge In The Four Noble Truths," I share my personal experience of contracting COVID and how embracing the Four Noble Truths guided me through recovery. This journey underscores the importance of self-compassion and resilience in the face of adversity.

Both talks emphasise that compassion is not merely an abstract concept but a practical tool that will transform our personal and professional lives. By cultivating compassion, we can navigate challenges with grace, build stronger connections, and lead with authenticity. These experiences have developed an assurance that compassion is the foundation upon which we can build a more empathetic and understanding world.

Compassion heals. It amplifies courage, clarity, and conviction. It reminds us that we are never truly alone in our struggles.

REFLECTION QUESTIONS

When was the last time someone showed you deep compassion, and how did it change you?

How do you respond when you are hurting—do you allow yourself care, or do you resist it?

What would it feel like to give compassion without expecting anything in return?

Chapter 28. Equanimity: A Mind That Is Peaceful In The Storm

Storms are never polite. They never knock, they never ask—they just show up, uninvited and unapologetic. For me, the storm was an ICU bed, an oxygen mask pressing against my face like it wanted to pick a fight, and the suffocating dread that every breath might be my last. Panic? Oh, it never tiptoed in—it charged through the door, yelling, "Let's see how much you can take!" My body was a warzone, my mind spiralling, emotions crashing into each other, creating chaos.

This was not my first storm. Life had been hurling curveballs at me for years—failures that stung like a slap, losses that felt like gut punches, and rejections that left me questioning my worth. But this storm, the ICU storm, was different. It stripped me of everything—control, strength, even dignity. And yet, in the middle of all that chaos, something unexpected stirred. Not peace, not calm—but a small, silent voice whispering: "Be here. Just be here."

Equanimity did not arrive as a grand revelation or a dramatic rescue. It was subtle. A calm presence—not loud, not forceful—but quietly steady. It was the ability to sit in the mess, fully aware of the pain and uncertainty, and choosing not to let it consume me. Equanimity is not floating above problems like some enlightened figure; it is standing in the centre of the storm—drenched, battered, but unbroken.

Let me tell you, in that ICU, panic was relentless. It whispered poison: "This is it. You're done for. Give up." Equanimity did not silence it. Instead, it nudged me gently and said, "Breathe. Now. Just breathe." It was not a profound insight. It was a deep soothing balm—the kind that keeps you alive when everything else fails.

We are often taught to resist storms, to fight, to conquer. But storms never care about resistance. They thrive on it. Equanimity teaches something different: "Let the storm rage. You? Just stay." It is about surrendering but never being consumed by the chaos. And if you are consumed, it reminds you, this too shall pass.

Equanimity takes strength. Real strength. It is the quiet power to stay when everything urges you to run. To acknowledge the storm without becoming it. To trust that even in the darkest moments, you have the capacity to remain present, steady, and whole.

In that ICU, my only focus became staying with each breath. No heroics. No profound realisations. Just the act of breathing—moment by moment. Equanimity is not about stopping the storm. It is about not letting the storm break you, and even if it breaks you, it is just another experience. It is the steady pulse that says, "I am still here."

EXPLORATION TIME
How can you cultivate equanimity when life feels overwhelming or painful or suffering?

Acknowledge the storm without resisting it. Acceptance never means giving up—it means recognising the reality of chaos without letting it define you.

Ground yourself in the present. Use breathwork, grounding techniques, and sensory awareness to stay connected to the moment.

Practice radical acceptance. Embrace discomfort as part of the human experience rather than forcing to eliminate it.

The thing about equanimity is that it makes you brave. It helps you show up, even when you are trembling, even when you have no answers. It helps you endure the storm not by overpowering it, but by refusing to be consumed by it. Equanimity is not passive—it is power in its purest form. The quiet, unwavering strength to stay.

When I think of or am touched by equanimity, it reminds me of my dear friend Alpesh. I never miss much about the UK, but I deeply miss Alpesh. He is an angel of compassion, a quiet anchor of equanimity. His presence feels like an unshakable calm, a space where chaos does not reach. Yes, he has his chaos to deal with, and yet he smiles. He never offers words of wisdom to pacify but radiates a depth of compassion that speaks louder than language.

Watching him move through life's uncertainties, steady and grounded, has shown me that equanimity is not about detachment from struggle—it is about embracing it with grace, staying present without becoming lost in the storm. His quiet strength has been a reminder that true equanimity is not perfection but the courage to remain open, vulnerable, and balanced, even when life feels unbearable.

Equanimity will not calm the storm, but it will keep the storm from breaking you. And in that stillness, in that unshakable centre yet flexible, is where your real power lies.

REFLECTION QUESTIONS
When was the last time you faced chaos and still managed to stay present?
How do you respond when life feels overwhelming? Do you resist, or do you allow yourself to be with the discomfort?

What practices can you adopt to cultivate greater equanimity in your daily life?

Chapter 29. Be Like Water: Mind-flow, Not Mindset

Water. It is the most unassuming force on Earth, yet it carves mountains and shapes landscapes. It adapts to its environment—soft and yielding when needed, but relentless and unyielding when necessary. In the ICU, I came to understand this truth intimately. My body was failing, my mind was spiralling, and yet, somewhere in the chaos, I realised that resisting was futile. If I was going to survive, I needed to stop fighting the current and start flowing with it.

Mindset. For me, it is a buzzword. Of course, structured thinking has its place—when learning new skills, mastering techniques, or building discipline. But when it comes to navigating life's uncertainties, mindsets fall short. They lock you into rigid patterns. Life demands something more fluid.

Everyone talks about having the right mindset—fixed mindset, growth mindset, winner's mindset. But here is the problem: a mindset is rigid by definition. It is literally set in its ways. It is a container, and containers are restrictions, with solid boundaries and walls. What I discovered in that ICU bed, gasping for breath, was that survival and growth require something more fluid. Something that cannot shatter under pressure. Something like water.

This is mind-flow.

Mindflow, Mind Flow, and Mind-Flow are the same concept, simply written with slight variations in spelling. All three describe the natural, uninterrupted movement of thoughts, emotions, and awareness through the mind. They reflect a state where mental activity flows freely without resistance, overthinking, or emotional turbulence. This mental state supports clarity, emotional balance, and a sense of calm presence.

This is distinct from Flow, as defined by Mihaly Csikszentmihalyi in the 1970s. His concept describes a task-focused state of deep immersion where an individual experiences effortless engagement and heightened productivity.

While flow focuses on peak performance during activities, mind-flow emphasises the smooth flow of inner thoughts and emotional clarity, allowing one to stay present and adaptable during life's storms.
Now, let me confess something: I have been a massive Bruce Lee fan since my childhood. I grew up watching his movies, thinking I was the next martial arts hero, side-kicking my way through imaginary enemies while the Kung Fu Fighting song played in the background. Of course, in reality, I was more like the clumsy extra who gets knocked out in the first five seconds of the movie—but hey, the spirit was there.

Bruce Lee had it right when he said, "Be water, my friend." Water does not fight obstacles; it flows around them. It does not resist change; it embraces it. It can crash, and it can calm, but it never loses its essence. His philosophy of fluidity stayed with me for years, but it was in the ICU that his words took on a whole new meaning—not just as wisdom, but as a survival principle.

Even Lao Tzu saw this thousands of years ago. "The highest good is like water. It benefits all things and does not compete." Water takes the lowest place, yet nothing overcomes it. It adapts, not out of weakness, but because it knows its power.

Modern thinkers echo this truth too. Raymond Tang, in his talk on Taoist wisdom, breaks it down into H2O—Humility, Openness, and Opportunity. Water stays humble, never forcing itself into spaces where it does not belong. It remains open, absorbing what it needs without resistance. And it finds opportunity where others see obstacles—flowing around, though, or over barriers, never stopping. That is exactly what mind-flow is about—not gripping so tightly that you break but moving in a way that keeps you standing.

In the ICU, my mind wanted to resist. It demanded answers, control, a way out. But water never argues with the riverbank. It never demands certainty. It simply flows. Mind-flow taught me to let go of my obsession with controlling the uncontrollable and instead focus on what I could do—take one breath, then another. Let my body do its thing, let the doctors and nurses do theirs, and trust the current.

It was Bruce Lee's words echoing in the back of my mind that shifted my perspective. I did not need to resist the storm. I needed to be like water—moving with it, not against it. His philosophy became more than a childhood admiration. It became a lifeline, reminding me that fluidity is not about weakness—it is about adaptability, strength, and resilience.

And before you ask—no, this was not some zen-like, monk-level enlightenment where I was floating above my body in complete peace. More like, "Oh no, am I about to die? Wait… okay… breathe."

Mind-flow is never about feeling calm all the time. It is about choosing not to fight the current, even when the waters are choppy.

Mind-flow is never about passivity. It is never about giving up. It is about being present. It is about understanding that life never moves in a straight line, and success is never a ladder you climb—it is a meandering river you navigate. Sometimes, the current will carry you effortlessly. Other times, you will need to paddle like hell. But either way, you keep moving.

EXPLORATION TIME
How could you cultivate mind-flow when life feels yuck?

Stop gripping the riverbank. The more you resist, the more you suffer. Release the need for control and flow with what is happening. Holding on too tightly breaks you under pressure.

Stay adaptable. Water changes form—ice, steam, liquid. Be flexible enough to shift your perspective when life demands it.

Breathe and observe. When chaos hits, come back to your breath. Notice the storm without becoming it

Release perfection. Water never stresses about being perfect. It flows. Do the same—progress, not perfection.

Trust the current. Life moves, even when you feel stuck. Trust that the flow will carry you forward, even when you cannot see the destination.

Let me ask you this: When life throws you into chaos, do you stiffen up, or do you flow? Rigidity breaks under pressure. Fluidity adapts and survives. Mind-flow is about being like water—resilient, adaptable, and true to your essence.

Being like water is what allows you to navigate uncertainty with grace, to find solutions where others see walls, and to keep moving forward when everything feels stuck. Mind-flow is never mindset—it is a way of being. And it is the key to living a life that does not just survive the storms but thrives in them.

The thing about mind-flow is that it turns you into a quiet powerhouse. It makes you adaptable, resilient, and anti-fragile. It whispers, "Keep moving," when life pins you down. And let's be honest—Bruce Lee would approve.

Be like water. Crash if you must. Flow when you can. But whatever you do—keep moving.

REFLECTION QUESTIONS:
When have you resisted life's currents instead of flowing with them? What did it cost you?
How can you practice mind-flow in areas where you currently feel stuck?
What would being more fluid and adaptable look like in your everyday challenges?

Part V: Money, Power, and Freedom

Money. Power. Freedom. They have been around for as long as humans have been breathing. They have built kingdoms and crumbled empires, lifted people to greatness, and left others gasping in the dirt. Love them, hate them, but one thing is for sure—you cannot ignore them. They are woven into the fabric of life itself, whether we like it or not.

Money whispers promise of security, of better days ahead. Power seduces with the allure of control, the chance to make the world bend to your will. Freedom? It teases us with endless possibilities, daring us to reach for more.

But here is the punchline: are we really free? Everything in life is interdependent—our success, our happiness, even our survival depends on someone, somewhere, showing up.

Freedom is an illusion, but collaboration is the key. Here on Earth, our lives are woven together by interdependence—our success, happiness, and

survival rely on the strength of those connections. For every step forward they offer, they demand something in return—your time, your energy, sometimes even your soul.

This is not about painting them as villains or saviours. They are neither. They are tools, weapons, lifelines, and chains—all at once. Part IV was about navigating the storms within—courage, clarity, conviction, and compassion. Now, we step into the external world, where money, power, and freedom reign supreme. They are the forces that shape our choices and challenge our values. They are both the dream and the distraction.

Money can be a lifeline or a trap, depending on how tightly you grip it. Power, when used with compassion, can transform lives; without it, it can destroy them. And freedom? It is not the fantasy of endless options. True freedom is finding peace within the confines life inevitably imposes.

Let us not romanticise these forces or vilify them. Let us understand them. Because here is the truth: they never need define you—unless you let them.

The real question is, what do they mean to you? Are they tools you wield, or masters you serve? Are they empowering you, or are they pulling your strings? Part V is not here to give you answers. It is here to make you uncomfortable, to hold up a mirror, to force you to confront your relationship with money, power, and freedom. Are they friends, foes, or something in between? That is for you to decide.

Welcome to Part V: Money, Power, and Freedom. Let us dive into this beauty.

Chapter 30. Money: A Friend, A Foe, or Both?

Money. It is everywhere—people enjoying it, slipping through our fingers, sitting smugly in someone else's pocket, whispering promises of happiness while taunting us with its absence. If money could talk, it would probably laugh at us for chasing it so relentlessly, then demand a tip for the trouble.

From the age of ten, I started working because I saw how much it helped when my parents struggled. Whether it was selling unwanted items from my father's shop to classmates, scraping coins from under vending machines, or earning approximately GBP 10 a week delivering newspapers, I learned early that money is not paper and metal. It is a tool—a way to move beyond surviving into striving and thriving, and yes, sometimes power.

During my younger years, living in a household of nine people, I often found myself cleaning out the sewage when it got blocked. To call a professional was a costly affair for the family, so I covered myself in literal shit, doing the cleanup manually. Years later, after graduating, while waiting for a graduate job, I worked as a security guard—because waiting for the perfect job would not pay the bills.

Money, like energy, can be directed with intention—toward growth, security, or even self-destruction, depending on the stories we attach to it. If you are generous, it lets you give more; if you are insecure, it whispers paranoia. But for a ten-year-old scraping coins from vending machines, money was not energy—it was survival wrapped in metal and paper.

By the time I was 23, with encouragement from my first wife and my father-in-law, I had bought my own apartment with a mortgage. I was rejecting job offers from well-known branded companies with low salaries and negligible career progression. Those offers were slave labour, where they arrogantly flaunted their name as if it were payment enough.

Money was never about luxury—it was about freedom, independence, and making sure my parents never felt like they had to support me. Every career move, every raise, every thoughtful decision about work—it was all about building something that felt secure.

But security is a double-edged sword. When I lost my job in my mid 20s, it shattered me. Redundancy hit like a freight train, but what lingered far worse was the shame. I had tied so much of my identity to being the provider. My self-worth was shackled to my income, and when the pay checks stopped, so did my belief in myself.

This pain rippled into my marriage. The fear of not being enough bit at me, and I responded by obsessing over how to fix it—chasing income instead of emotional connection. My inability to express vulnerability—my belief that love was earned through financial stability—pushed her away. I was drowning, yet too proud to ask for help, convinced that if I was not providing, I was failing.

Even now, the thought of financial instability lingers somewhere deep in my subconscious. Perhaps it stems from my childhood, where I experienced only lack. Money was always a point of contention—fuel for family fights, a reason we never went on vacations or entertained ourselves, a loud force that made asking for a treat feel like begging for scraps. Yes, it was poverty in mind and poverty in action. Those early memories left a mark, shaping how I view and feel about money even today.

Many times, my loved ones urge me to invest so I can experience further financial growth like they do. Their suggestions include property or another business. I refuse. Why? The risk. Taking a loan or borrowing money has always felt dangerous. The idea of being in debt again, of possibly failing to repay it, stirs an old fear—the same one that once kept me awake at night when I was struggling to keep up with basic living expenses.

That fear is not irrational, is it? It is ancient, primal, woven from past wounds where scarcity was not just a thought but a physical reality. The nights of counting coins, balancing on the edge of survival—these moments leave echoes. And such echoes do not fade easily when they have shaped who you had to become.

Yet, here lies the truth I already knew but resisted saying aloud: fear protects as much as it confines. It once kept me alert, made me move, ensured I never slipped back into that abyss of financial strain. But somewhere along the way, it overstayed its welcome. It became the wall instead of the armour.

When my loved ones urge me to invest, they do not just see numbers. They see potential. But for me, it is different. Borrowing is not a strategy—it is a reminder. A confrontation with a version of myself who once felt powerless. And the most haunting part? I know I could survive it all over again, yet I no longer wish to test my capacity for survival.

It is not weakness. It is exhaustion.

Perhaps the deeper truth is this: my fear is not about debt. It is the fear of losing control again. Of being at the mercy of circumstances I cannot bend with sheer willpower. And so, I avoid risk—not because I lack courage but because I know too intimately the cost of failure.

What if the answer is not in silencing the fear but in understanding it better? Not all risks are reckless. Not all caution is paralysis. Maybe the fear is asking me to slow down—not stop completely. To choose what I invest in with intention, not avoidance.

The question is no longer whether fear is valid—it is. The question is whether it still serves me or if it now holds me captive to a version of myself I have long outgrown. I have already proven I can survive, strive and thrive. Now, can I trust myself to amplify thriving?

EXPLORATION TIME
How could you redefine your relationship with money?

Explore the origins of your money beliefs. Reflect on childhood experiences and cultural messages that shaped your relationship with money. Identify which beliefs still serve you and which need to be released.

Shift from scarcity to value. When making financial decisions, ask: "Am I choosing from fear or value?" Focus on how money can support your growth, not control your life.

Practice financial mindfulness. Track your spending with curiosity, not judgment. Notice patterns and how they reflect your emotional state rather than external needs.

Clarify the role of money in your life. Write down what money represents for you—freedom, security, power? Challenge yourself to find non-financial sources for these feelings as well.

Give without attachment. Whether it is donating or helping a friend, give from a place of care without expecting anything in return, allowing money to flow freely instead of clinging to it.

Here is what I have learned: Money is not the root of all evil, nor is it salvation. It is energy—a powerful force that reflects the intentions behind its use. Respect it, value it, and understand its ability to amplify both good and harm. But remember, it is not money that corrupts—it is how we use it and what we let it mean to us.

It is not a god, and it is not a devil. It is a tool. It amplifies who you are. If you are generous, money lets you give more. If you are insecure, money makes you more paranoid. Once again, it is not money itself—it is the stories we attach to it.

Respect money. Value it. See it for what it is: energy, potential, a means to create joy and share love. When approached with equanimity, money becomes powerful in the best way. But when tied to fear, greed, or guilt, it poisons everything it touches.

Either way, treat money kindly and with respect. After all, if money talks, you might as well make it say something nice.

REFLECTION QUESTIONS:
What is your earliest memory of money, and how has it shaped your beliefs today?

*How do you currently define financial success,
and does it align with your core values?
What would it feel like to approach money as a
tool for freedom rather than a measure of worth?*

Chapter 31: Freedom Is In Acceptance

The idea of independence is one of the biggest scams life throws at us. The scam is promoted by media, motivational providers, manifestation teachers, and many more who see this as a money-making opportunity. "Stand tall, stand alone," they say. Really? Have you ever made it through a day without relying on someone or something? No coffee, no Wi-Fi, no electricity, not even a kind word from a stranger. That is what the illusion of independence looks like—impossible and impractical.

Independence is shaky, impractical, and, frankly, a lie we keep telling ourselves. Life, messy and absurd as it is, keeps slapping us with the truth: freedom has nothing to do with cutting ties. It comes from realising how gloriously interconnected we are with others and learning to dance with grace in the chaos of life.

We are not independent; we are gloriously, beautifully, ridiculously interdependent. You, me, the barista making your coffee, the tree outside your

window, the oxygen filling your lungs—we are all part of this wild web. Relationships, work, family, even the air we breathe ties us to others in ways we rarely stop to consider. Embracing this is not a loss of freedom; it is the key to discovering it.

Take emotions. We like to think our feelings belong to us alone, yet research proves otherwise. When someone laughs or cries, your brain lights up as if you are feeling it too. We are hardwired for connection, whether we like it or not.

I learned this painfully through my loved ones. There have been moments where I had to step back, letting them make their choices—even when every fibre of my being screamed to intervene. To fix. To protect them from mistakes I believed were inevitable.

What happened next was humbling. They owned their choices, faced the consequences with courage, and emerged stronger. Watching them, I realised how much I had underestimated them. The experience never weakened our bond—it tightened it, like a knot drawn tighter under pressure. That is what interdependence means. It is not control. It is being there—to guide when asked, to catch when necessary, and often, to step back and trust.

Then there is work. Every time I speak on a stage, the success of that moment is never mine alone. Before I ever face an audience, someone adjusts the mic, tests the lighting, fine-tunes the sound. Without them, I am just a man talking to himself in the dark. They are the silent architects of the moment—unseen, yet essential.

This is the truth in every industry. No success, no achievement, no great victory happens solo. Every result is the product of countless contributions—most invisible, yet profoundly significant. The myth of the self-made success story? Pure fiction. Life is a shared masterpiece.

Even nature understands this. Trees breathe out oxygen, which we inhale, while we exhale carbon dioxide, feeding the trees. The cycle sustains life itself. Ecosystems thrive not in isolation but through collaboration. Yet, we forget this fundamental truth—

until crisis hits. A pandemic. A natural disaster. A sudden loss. And suddenly, we remember how dependent we are on each other, on systems we rarely notice until they fail.

And then there is family. Blood means nothing without joy, love, and compassion. My former wife's family taught me this. They showed me what genuine support looks like—standing by me without toxic conditions, without expectation of gain. Their care was not transactional. It was love in its rawest, purest form.

They taught me something profound: Family is never defined by genetics but by those who show up. It is built on trust, kindness, and the willingness to stand with someone, even when there is nothing to gain.

John Donne wrote, "No man is an island." His words remain timeless—no one thrives in isolation. True freedom does not arise from standing alone but from recognising the strength that comes through connection. We are part of something larger than ourselves, woven into an intricate web where each thread strengthens the whole.

Spiritually, this wisdom echoes across traditions. Buddhism speaks of interbeing—the idea that all things exist in relationship to everything else. No flower blooms without the sun. No sun without the universe. Indigenous cultures have long understood that humans are not separate from the earth but caretakers within a vast living system.

This truth is not just poetic—it is practical. When we release the illusion that strength means standing alone, we discover a deeper freedom. A freedom found in knowing we are never truly alone.

EXPLORATION TIME

How can you embrace the power of interdependence?

Reflect on the ways you are currently interdependent on others and express gratitude for their support.

Identify one area where you have resisted asking for help and challenge yourself to reach out.

Have a conversation with someone who has supported you and acknowledge their impact on your life.

Explore a philosophical tradition like Buddhism or Stoicism to deepen your understanding of interdependence.

Create a visual representation of your support network—whether a mind map or journal entry—and reflect on its strength.

When we let go of the illusion that strength means standing alone, we begin to discover a deeper truth. Our shared existence is messy, magnificent, and meaningful precisely because of the ways we depend on each other.

Leaning on others never makes you weak—it makes you human. Strength is not about pretending you can handle everything on your own. That is a lie we tell ourselves to feel in control, but it is exhausting, and it breaks you. Real strength is knowing when to say, "I cannot do this alone." It is letting someone else carry the load when you are about to collapse.

It is messy, uncomfortable, and yes, sometimes it feels like failure. But it is not. It is survival. The truth is none of us make it through this life alone. We need each other—desperately, awkwardly, beautifully. So, stop clinging to the illusion of independence and let yourself lean, even if it feels like falling. That is where the real strength lives.

Freedom is never found in the illusion of independence. It is discovered in the messy, magnificent truth of our shared existence—where every thread strengthens the fabric and every connection adds meaning

REFLECTION QUESTIONS:
Where in your life have you confused independence with strength, and how has it limited you?

What would change if you fully embraced the idea of interdependence?

Who in your life deserves more acknowledgment for the role they play in your growth and freedom?

Chapter 32: When Forgiveness Feels Impossible

Forgiveness—a word so heavy it feels like a command rather than an invitation. "You should forgive," they say, as if the act is simple, as if you can wave a wand over your pain and make it disappear. But what about when forgiveness feels like betrayal? What about when it feels impossible?

I know that impossibility well. Forgiving my former wife was not a decision made overnight. It began as a begrudging thought, a hesitant crack in the wall of my resentment. The pain of our separation, the sense of betrayal, the questions that echoed long after we parted—they clung to me like a second skin. Letting go of that pain felt like tearing off my armour. Armour, I thought was protecting me, but in truth, it was toxic, corroding me from the inside. It felt safer to stay guarded, to let the bitterness define me.

Forgiveness came slowly, not as some noble gesture but as a survival decision. Holding onto the resentment felt like drinking poison and hoping she would suffer. It never worked. Forgiving her did not erase the past or absolve her actions; it simply freed me from carrying their weight every single day. Each step forward felt unsteady, but with every piece of pain I released, I began to breathe a little deeper. I began to reclaim my wholesome self.

Nothing prepared me for the challenge of forgiving my parents. They are beautiful people, full of love and sacrifices. Yet, their pain, their unhealed wounds, spilled over into my life. Forgiveness here was never about excusing harm but about acknowledging their humanity while allowing myself the space to heal. Forgiving them was never about erasing the scars. It was about releasing the weight so I could finally step into my truth.

Yet, despite understanding this intellectually, I have still not found full peace with my parents. The emotional residue lingers, a sign that I need to go deeper, that forgiveness is not yet complete in my heart. Karma feels present here encouraging me to compassionately resolve it. It is a reminder that forgiveness is not a decision; it is a lifelong process that demands courage and honesty with oneself.

What makes forgiveness so hard? It is more than the act of letting go. It is the fear that forgiving will somehow invalidate your pain. That it might minimise what happened. Forgiveness feels impossible when you think it means making excuses for those who hurt you. It is not about excusing. It is about refusing to let your pain be the lens through which you view life.

And then, there are those you cannot, and should not, let back into your life. The abusers. The manipulators. The ones who refuse to take accountability and continue to harm. Forgiveness here is not an invitation for them to return—it is a shield. Forgiveness does not mean handing them power again. It means releasing their grip on your mind. It means saying, "You will not live rent-free in my heart anymore."

But what do you do when abusers—those unrelated to the love and care of your parents or other loved ones—never let you off? When they thrive on control, chasing you to hell and back, not for reconciliation but to teach you a lesson for standing up to them? When they refuse accountability and find allies to justify their harm? Forgiveness here is not about handing them power—it means setting shields so strong they cannot breach them. Forgiveness becomes about releasing their power over your mind, not reopening wounds or inviting continued harm. It is self-respect in its highest form.

Cutting toxic cycles is not about cruelty. It is about self-respect. Toxic people thrive on control, guilt, and emotional entanglement. Forgiveness is not letting them back in—it is raising a shield while releasing the emotional burden of their actions. Some people are meant to be forgiven from a distance. Their pain has roots, but so does yours, and shielding yourself from continued harm is not cruelty—it is wisdom.

We often label others as toxic without acknowledging that the most relentless critic often lives within us. Who has echoed the harshest words in your mind during moments of self-doubt? Who has clung to past mistakes and replayed them on repeat? The struggle, the flaws you wish to erase, are not poison. They are parts of you asking for compassion, not exile. Cutting the cycle means breaking free from both external harm and internal self-judgment—not severing every connection but healing the patterns that have kept you trapped.

Forgiveness, however, is never a race. It is neither a checklist nor a deadline. It is a process—messy, uneven, and painfully slow. There will be days when you feel like you have let go, only to be blindsided by an old memory that rips the wound open again. And that is okay. Forgiveness is about progress. It is about choosing, again and again, to put down the weight—even when part of you still wants to hold it.

EXPLORATION TIME:
How can you begin releasing the weight of unforgiveness?

Identify the emotional roots. Reflect on a past hurt and name the emotions it still stirs in you. Acknowledge how those feelings shape your present mind.

Write a raw, unfiltered letter. Without sending it, express every emotion you have toward the person you struggle to forgive—especially the unspoken pain.

Establish shields. Protect yourself from those who continue to harm you. Shields are not walls. They are acts of self-respect, ensuring your emotional safety.

Release the need for closure. Stop waiting for the other person to change. Acceptance never requires reconciliation.

Turn inward with compassion. Forgive yourself for holding onto pain. Speak kindly to yourself as you heal, releasing guilt for not having healed sooner.

Forgiveness can feel like climbing a mountain with no summit. Some days, you will stop. Some days, you will slip backward. And that is human. There is no shame in admitting the climb feels impossible. The strength lies in the fact that you keep showing up, even when the pain feels unbearable.

Forgiveness never rewrites the past. It does not erase what happened. It reclaims your peace. It is not about letting someone off the hook—it is about letting yourself off the hook from carrying their weight. And while it may feel impossible, the smallest step toward forgiveness begins to shift everything.

Forgiveness is never about perfection. It is not a moral checklist. It is untidy. Personal. Sometimes agonising. Yet every time you face it, no matter how imperfectly, you loosen the grip the past has on your present. You move closer to freedom.

REFLECTION QUESTIONS:
What belief about forgiveness has been holding you back from healing?
How can you raise emotional shields while still releasing emotional burdens?
What would it feel like to release the pain you have carried for so long?

Chapter 33: Navigating the Space Between Holding On and Letting Go

Navigating the space between holding on and letting go depends entirely on the situation. Maybe it is waiting for a client who promises they will get back to you but never does, leaving you in limbo. Or it is holding onto hope that an intimate partner will change, convincing yourself that patience and gratitude will turn things around.

You wait, and wait, until frustration builds like magma under a volcano. When nothing changes, you explode—maybe in private, maybe at someone else. Then comes the regret. Why did I not let go sooner? And why do I keep holding on?

Sometimes it feels like being stuck in a queue that never moves. You tell yourself, "Just a little longer," but the wait stretches endlessly. The frustration eats at you, and you start questioning if staying was ever the right choice.

Other times, holding on feels like gripping sand slipping through your fingers. You wonder if letting go will bring relief or regret, leaving you torn between the fear of losing something valuable and the hope of finding something better. It is not about knowing the outcome—it is about finding the courage to act despite the uncertainty.

We often glorify holding on, wrapping it in words like loyalty, strength, or persistence. But let us be honest—many times holding on is fear disguised as strength. It is clutching onto a relationship, an idea, or even an outdated version of yourself because letting go feels like losing control. And letting go? It never feels like a triumphant moment. Sometimes it is ugly tears streaming, chest tight, wondering if you have just made the biggest mistake of your life. But on those rare occasions when you finally let go, it feels like a weight has been lifted, even if just for a moment.

The aftermath never feels tidy. Some days, letting go feels like freedom—like exhaling after holding your breath for too long. Other days, sadness lingers, making you second-guess everything. And then there are the confusing days where it is all a mix, and you are left trying to pick up the pieces.

Deciding what to let go of and what to keep is a minefield. I have clung to people and memories like they were lifelines, only to realise they were anchors dragging me under. I have let go of things that felt like pieces of my soul, and it hurt—deeply. For many, clarity never comes easily. Sometimes it takes weeks, months, or even years. And in that time, we make mistakes, cause hurt, and are left with regret. But on those rare occasions, something shifts. It feels as though something inside whispers, "This is the way," and suddenly, clarity emerges.

This is never straightforward. One day you are convinced you have moved on, and the next, you are peeling back a new layer of unresolved feelings. It is not about getting over it but getting through it, piece by piece.

The truth is chaos never fully disappears. Over the years, I have explored countless tools to navigate it—

cognitive behaviour techniques, logical and rational frameworks, meditation, journaling, reiki, pranic healing, and many others. Yes, they help in their own ways. For me, only a few tools have consistently worked most effectively. The mantra of Nirvana Shatakam, Ho'oponopono by Morrnah Simeona, and the gentle guidance of Thich Nhat Hanh's voice saying, "Just breathe," have been my true anchors. They calm the storm, create space for clarity, and remind me that even amidst chaos, there is a way forward.

Cutting toxic cycles also plays a crucial role here. When you hold onto relationships or situations that repeatedly cause harm, holding on is no longer strength—it is self-sabotage. Cutting toxic cycles does not mean cutting people out of your life with cruelty. It means releasing patterns where pain, guilt, and emotional control keep you tethered. Letting go is not abandonment; it is self-respect.

EXPLORATION TIME
How can you begin navigating the space between holding on and letting go?

Identify the emotional roots. Reflect on a situation where you feel stuck. Is your attachment driven by hope, fear, or obligation? Acknowledge the discomfort without judgment.

Write a letter of release. Without sending it, express every unspoken thought and pain you have been carrying about what you struggle to release. Let it be unfiltered and raw.

Clarify what holding on has cost you. Identify the emotional, mental, physical and spiritual toll it has taken on your well-being. What are you sacrificing by not letting go?

Experiment with symbolic release. Physical acts of release—burning the letter, closing a chapter with a ritual, or physically stepping away from situations that drain you.

Raise shields when necessary. If a person or situation continues to harm you, focus on emotional shielding instead of self-blame. Forgiveness never means re-entry into harm.

Letting go is never a perfect process. It is disorganised, uncomfortable, and often feels like a contradiction of strength and vulnerability. Yet, the courage to release what no longer serves you is the foundation of healing.

For me, and for many others I know, letting go has been damn tough. When my six-year relationship with a woman I deeply loved ended abruptly because that was what she wanted, it wrecked me. I wanted answers. I wanted to know what went wrong, to analyse every word, every moment, every choice I made. But she cut me off like a limb infected with gangrene—severed, because it was easier to remove than to heal. No explanation, no closure—just brutal silence. Oh, the dreams of building a family, of sharing a life, shattered in seconds. To this day, I have no idea why she walked away.

And then, I have found myself in a situationship. Another lesson in letting go, but this time, it came fast and heartless. The behaviour from the other side screamed of unresolved trauma—a textbook case if you go by Dr. John Gottman's research. She clung to her pain like a brick wall, refusing to let it go, and I had to accept that.

It is not just relationships, either. It is when clients ghost me after promises made or when family members hit me with something sensitive, something they know will cut deep. It gets to me every time. And as I get older, I am slowly realising the truth we all run from: humans are selfish. We are messy bags of emotions, stuck in our own stories, blind to the damage we leave behind. We justify it, move on, and rarely stop to think about the karma of our ways and how it ripples out, wrecking others in ways we will never see.

Sometimes, navigating the space between holding on and letting go means recognising that both have value. Holding on teaches resilience. Letting go teaches surrender. Neither is easy. Both hurt. But in their own way, both show you what it means to be strong. Letting go teaches surrender.

Navigating the space between holding on and letting go is never about doing it right. It is about embracing the disorder, finding meaning in the

chaos, and letting every choice you make add another brushstroke to the masterpiece of your life.

REFLECTION QUESTIONS

What beliefs keep you holding on when it might be healthier to let go?

How can you begin releasing emotional weight without feeling like you are giving up?

What would trusting yourself to make the next decision feel like, even without complete clarity?

Chapter 34: Deep Listening: Two Ears, One Heart

Let me tell you a story. There was a time when my partner sat across from me, tears from her eyes. She spoke, her words halting and raw, and I, believing I was helping, began offering solutions. She stopped mid-sentence, looked at me, and said, "Can you just listen?" Her voice was not angry; it was exhausted. She did not want answers. She wanted presence. She wanted to feel heard. That moment shattered something in me—my assumption that love meant fixing. It was a hard, uncomfortable truth: love often means silence, presence, and the courage to hold space.

The word "heart" holds "ear" within it. This simple fact speaks volumes about the profound relationship between listening and connection. But how often do we truly listen? And when we do, are we listening with our ears alone, or with our entire being?

Listening is not comfortable. It is not easy. It asks for vulnerability—the courage to let go of your ego, to sit in the discomfort of someone else's pain, and to resist the urge to respond. True listening demands more than the physical act of hearing. It requires emotional openness, the capacity to witness without judgment, without interruption, without needing to steer the conversation back to yourself.

Here is the uncomfortable truth: we often listen to reply, not to understand. We fill silences with our assumptions, afraid of what might surface if we let them linger. But true listening lives in those silences. Silence is never empty; it is fertile ground where truths take root and grow.

Have you ever noticed the shape of an ear? It curves inward, resembling a womb—a space of receptivity and creation. The ear and the womb share a sacred role: they nurture what they receive. Just as the womb cradles life, the ear cradles stories, emotions, and truths. Listening is never passive; it actively shapes understanding, it sparks deeper insight and connection. It is part of the healing journey.

Now, imagine placing two ears side by side. Together, they form the shape of a heart. This is no coincidence. Listening is an act of love. It is the bridge between hearing and feeling, between sound and empathy. When we listen with our hearts, we do more than hear words; we absorb the emotions and intentions behind them. We step into another's world, even if only for a moment.

The song "The Living Years" by Mike and the Mechanics captures this sentiment beautifully: "You can listen as well as you hear." This line reminds us that listening is not merely about using our ears; it is about engaging with our entire being.

The ancient Chinese symbol for listening offers profound wisdom on this. It integrates six components: the ear for hearing, the eyes for observing body language, the heart for emotional understanding, undivided attention to stay fully present, and respect for treating the speaker as though they are the most important person in the world. Listening, in this sense, becomes a holistic act of connection.

Epictetus, the Greek Stoic philosopher, once enslaved, later exiled, understood listening as an act of power and wisdom. His words echo across centuries: "We have two ears and one mouth so that we can listen twice as much as we speak." This teaching challenges us to prioritise listening as a pathway to wisdom and compassion, urging us to let go of our obsession with being heard and focus instead on understanding.

Listening can be weaponised too. Emotional manipulators listen not to understand but to gather ammunition. Toxic listening is when someone only absorbs words to twist them, guilt-trip you, or maintain control. True listening, in contrast, never seeks power over someone. If you find yourself surrounded by those who listen only to control, the act of raising emotional shields becomes critical.

Cutting toxic cycles is not about cruelty. It is about self-respect. Some people use listening as a way to gather ammunition for future harm, twisting your vulnerability back at you. Forgiveness here does not mean re-entry into harm. It means recognising when someone uses your truth against you and choosing emotional safety over forced reconciliation. Set shields, not walls. Distance yourself from harmful dynamics while protecting your peace.

EXPLORATION TIME
How can you begin listening with your whole heart?

Pause before responding. Allow silence to create space for deeper truths instead of rushing to fill gaps with words. Notice the discomfort and stay with it.

Make eye contact and give full attention. Resist distractions and show the speaker that they matter deeply in that moment.

Ask open-ended questions. Use prompts like, "What else would you like to share?" or "How does this feel for you?" to encourage deeper expression without interruption.

Reflect back what you hear. Saying, "I hear you saying..." to clarify understanding and ensure the speaker feels heard.

Resist the urge to fix. Instead, offer validation: "That sounds incredibly difficult. I am here with you."

Listening with your heart is not without challenges. It requires courage. It demands that you stay present when every part of you wants to retreat. It asks you to put aside your need to fix, to advise, and instead offer presence. Listening is not about surrendering your truth but about creating a space where two truths can exist without conflict.

Listening also transforms us. It teaches humility. It shows us that we do not have all the answers, that sometimes the most profound act of love is to simply be there—without words, without solutions. Listening is about presence. It is about saying, "I am here with you," even when you do not know what to say.
This is deep listening.

Deep listening is the art of fully engaging with others—hearing not just their words, but their emotions and intentions. It's about being present, attentive, and open, creating a space where true understanding can flourish.

REFLECTION QUESTIONS

Think of a time when someone truly listened to you. How did it make you feel?

Who in your life is waiting for you to listen—not just with your ears, but with your heart?

What fears or assumptions hold you back from listening more deeply, and how might you overcome them?

Chapter 35: Humour: Laughing Through Life's Chaos

Humour never announces its arrival, nor does it wait for the perfect moment. It sneaks in like an old friend, bringing lightness when the air feels suffocating. In the middle of life's chaos, humour reminds us of something essential: we are still human. It is never a shield to block the storm but a bridge—connecting despair to hope, fragility to resilience, and suffering to compassion.

For me, humour has been this bridge many times. But no moment encapsulates its power more vividly than the time I was lying on my deathbed with COVID. Oxygen levels plummeted, pneumonia raged, and each breath was a battle. Yet, amidst this terrifying fragility, I felt an undeniable calling to play comedy clips in English, Hindi, Urdu, and Punjabi. Yes, even Korean, Japanese, Vietnamese, Malaysian and many more. None of it was calculated. None of it was a strategy. It was simply something I knew I had to do.

And so, in that sterile, beeping ICU, the sounds of laughter and absurdity mingled with the harsh rhythm of machines keeping me alive. Did the jokes cure me? No. Did they erase the pain? Absolutely not. But they shifted something primal—like a small ember of life flickering back to remind me I was still here. It felt ridiculous and profound all at once, as if laughter had the audacity to defy death itself.

The contrast was startling. On one side, the crushing weight of mortality pressing down on my chest. On the other, the absurd amusement of human existence. I felt my own laughter bubble up, surprising me. It was weak, fleeting, but undeniable. In that moment, humour was not just a distraction. It was a lifeline—a reminder of the absurdity, beauty, and unpredictability of life.

Humour acted like a quiet companion, sitting with me in the darkness, refusing to let me drown. At times, it softened the harshness of my reality, like a balm on raw skin. In other moments, it was a spark, jolting me awake and reminding me that amidst the chaos, life still had its rhythm—and that rhythm included laughter.

It was during this time I made the joyous discovery that humour, a smile, and laughter bring compassion to ease suffering. Humour became more than a coping mechanism; it was a force of healing, a rebellion against despair. It reminded me that the presence of pain did not cancel out the right to experience joy.

Let us be clear: humour never erases suffering. Real humour, the kind that cracks you open, is not avoidance—it is a refusal to be consumed by darkness. It is a quiet act of defiance. Humour never dismisses pain. It sits beside it, making space for both grief and joy to coexist.

It taught me the importance of being comfortable in my own company. Being alone never meant being lonely. Loneliness is a void echoing with disconnection, but solitude—when held with kindness—offers healing. Humour helped me reconnect with myself in those quiet moments, not to distract from the pain but to hold it gently.

And humour ripples outward. The energy in that hospital room shifted. Nurses who were overworked and emotionally exhausted would sometimes pause to listen to the jokes playing. Their muffled laughter behind the masks told me something powerful: humour did not only serve me—it became a bridge between people, a shared human release.

Yet, humour has its shadows too. There is the kind of humour that mocks, belittles, or deflects. Sarcasm disguised as humour that cuts deep or forced positivity that denies genuine emotion. Toxic humour dismisses pain instead of holding it. Healing humour, on the other hand, acknowledges reality while offering space for relief.

And there is the other side—when laughter becomes a shield, blocking vulnerability. Joking away trauma. Hiding behind humour instead of facing the discomfort of unresolved pain. Real humour never masks reality; it reveals it with tenderness.

EXPLORATION TIME

How can you begin using humour as a bridge, not a distraction?

Recall a painful memory where humour softened the pain. Reflect on how laughter shifted the emotional weight in that moment.

Expose yourself to conscious humour. Watch or read something that makes you genuinely laugh—without guilt—and notice how it affects your emotional clarity.

Share laughter with intention. Share a funny memory during a difficult conversation and observe how it shifts the emotional energy between you and the other person.

Laugh at your imperfections. Instead of judging your flaws, use humour as a way to embrace your humanity without self-punishment.

Keep a 'humour journal'. Document moments of laughter that have lightened your heart and revisit them when life feels heavy.

Humour never erases your struggles, nor does it solve your problems. But it becomes a bridge—a momentary crossing from despair to hope, from isolation to connection, from chaos to clarity. It is a quiet ally, a spark in the darkness, and a profound reminder of what it means to be human.

So, embrace the chaos and let humour walk with you. Laugh at the absurdity, smile at the unpredictability, and let the power of humour guide you through life's messiest moments.

When you laugh, even for a second, you reclaim a part of yourself that chaos cannot touch.

REFLECTION QUESTIONS:
Think of a time when laughter helped you navigate a difficult moment. What did it shift for you?

How does humour connect you to others, even in times of struggle?

What role does laughter play in your journey of rediscovering resilience and humanity?

Chapter 36: The Trap of Comparison

I was four years old when it began. British-born. The only one in an Indian boarding school. That fact alone made me a target.

Angrez. Gaddaar.

They spat the words at me like they were my name. But they were more than words—they were scars. Angrez meant foreigner. Gaddaar meant traitor. But in those corridors, it was not just language. It was a loaded accusation, soaked in bitterness I was too young to understand but old enough to feel pressing on my chest. I was not just different—I was wrong, simply for being born elsewhere.

The teachers said it too. They were not protectors. They were not neutral. They participated. I was not just called angrez gaddaar by children testing limits—I was called privileged by adults who should have known better. My birthplace wass treated as a sin I could never erase.

At first, it was words. Whispered. Spat. Hurled like stones. I stayed silent. Not because I was weak, but because I believed silence would stop the pain. But words, when left unchecked, do not disappear. They fester.

When words turned to hands—shoves, punches, strikes—I fought back. Not once did I throw the first punch. But when they hit me, I made sure they felt it back. And I paid for it.

The teachers never saw the first strike. But they saw my retaliation. And they punished me. Detention. Canes across my hands and body. Rulers slashing my palms and knuckles. They were not teaching me a lesson—they were breaking me.

School became a breeding ground for abuse—verbal, emotional, physical, even sexual. None of this made me bitter, but it did leave scars—beliefs designed to protect me but that instead sabotaged me. I have learned to be compassionate with myself, even when the shadows linger. But let us be honest—schools, families, societies, governments—they focus more on outward development, ignoring the silent wounds left unchecked.

You may wonder—Why not tell your parents? I did. And they thought I was lying. They believed the teachers. I was just a child. Authority figures were trusted more than my words. So, I stayed silent.

But the words never left me. Words wound in ways bruises never could. Bruises fade. Words linger. Words outlast pain. They burrow beneath the skin, wrapping around your heart, shaping how you see yourself long after the voices go quiet.

And this—this is where the poison of comparison began.

Not the kind that inspires growth. Not the kind that makes you strive for better. No. This was the kind that poisons. The kind that whispers: You will never be enough.

Comparison, by itself, is neutral. Like a knife—it can prepare a meal or cause harm. It depends on the intention behind it. But when comparison disconnects you from yourself, it turns toxic.

It poisons when it morphs into self-criticism—that relentless voice whispering, You will never measure up.

It poisons when it fuels resentment—Why do they deserve success more than me?

It poisons when it drives external validation—that endless hunger for approval, fed by the illusion that happiness lies in measuring up to others' standards.

Yet, comparison can also be a teacher. It can guide when approached with clarity and mindfulness. You compare career paths to assess which one aligns better with your values and skills. You compare relationships to understand what brings you genuine connection and emotional safety. Comparing can reveal areas where you desire growth or uncover personal values you had not clearly identified before. The difference lies in the intention behind the comparison.

When comparison disconnects you from compassion, it poisons. When comparison reconnects you to clarity, it encourages.

EXPLORATION TIME

How can you move away from toxic comparison?

Identify the source. Reflect on where toxic comparison first appeared in your life. Write down specific moments when you felt diminished by it.

Face the narrative. Identify whether the standards you compare yourself to were shaped by your truth or imposed by others. Ask, Who gave me this story?

Shift the focus. Instead of comparing your worth to others, focus on your personal growth and the progress you have made.

Practice self-compassion. Speak to yourself with the same care you would offer a dear friend.

Be aware of external triggers. Reduce exposure to media or environments that trigger toxic comparison and focus on spaces that celebrate authenticity.

Toxic comparing will never have a finishing line. It spreads across all types of media, influencing individuals, families, communities, cultures, governments, and entire nations. The system is rigged this way—designed to keep you constantly reaching, endlessly striving, forever feeling behind.

Someone will always have more. Someone will always seem further ahead. You were never meant to win the game. But here is the truth: You were never meant to play by their rules.

You never needed their approval. You never needed their standards. And the moment you stop measuring yourself against illusions and external noise, you reclaim the truth that was always yours.

You were never broken. You have always been enough.

REFLECTION QUESTIONS

Who first made you feel different, and how has it shaped your sense of self-worth today?

How has toxic comparison distorted your beliefs about yourself?

What would shift if you stopped measuring your life against others and focused on embracing your truth?

Chapter 37: Celebrate Failure, Your Greatest Painful Beautiful Teacher

I have been awarded multiple PhDs in failure—self-proclaimed, of course and also generously conferred by life itself and, let us be honest, by numerous critics since the moment I was born, all arriving in different shapes and sizes. Thank you for this wonderful honour. I truly appreciate it.

Failure. The word itself feels heavy, like a stone pressing against the chest. A punch to the gut. The unbearable pain. Yet here you are. Still breathing. Still standing. So, why do we treat failure like a scar that needs hiding? It is not the villain we have made it out to be. Failure is raw, revealing, and yes, painful. But it is also powerful. It can break you open and rebuild you stronger.

We have been raised with a lie. Life is neatly divided into two camps—success or failure. Pass or fail. Win or lose. Life painted in black and white. From our earliest memories, schools, parents, and the media—the conditioning starts early. Success is praised.

Failure is buried. We are taught to be ashamed of it, to feel guilty about it. But what if failure was never meant to break you? What if it was your most honest teacher?

From the moment we take our first breath, we are handed a label: 'Success' or 'failure.' It is like life's cruel game, and these titles mean absolutely nothing. From childhood to the grave, we collect them like trophies, chasing them, desperately trying to prove our worth.

Success is celebrated like a god, failure shamed like a curse. We are taught to crave success and fear failure. But here is the truth they will never tell you— these labels are empty. Hollow prizes handed to us by a world that never cared to know who we really are.

The reality is, we are more than our successes, more than our failures. These moments—these so-called accolades—should never define us. What defines us is how we rise after we fall, how we keep moving forward when the world tells us we are broken. Life is never black and white. It is not about winning or losing. It is about the mess in between—the parts of us that are not perfect, the failures we do our best to bury. And the most painful truth? It is in those failures that we find our strength. We learn from the scars we carry, from the times we thought we were done, only to rise again bruised but unbroken.

A story for you: Two men stood on the edge of a storm. One saw the clouds and charged straight in, determined to conquer it head-on. The other paused. He watched. Waited. Listened. Who was wiser? Toxic inspiration tells us to power through the storm, no matter the cost. Real wisdom, though, knows that sometimes you need to stop, breathe, and wait for the right moment. The world never celebrates the one who paused—but perhaps they should. Because reckless action is not courage. It is foolishness. And it has consequences.

Failure is uncomfortable because it strips away the illusion of control. It exposes the cracks we work so hard to hide. As the poet Rumi said, "The wound is the place where the light enters you." The cracks, the wounds—they are where the light breaks in. Thus, failure can never define you. It reveals you.

Confucius understood this long ago when he said, "By three methods we may learn wisdom: First, by reflection, which is the noblest; Second, by imitation, which is the easiest; And third, by experience, which is the bitterest."

Reflection allows us to learn by looking inward. Imitation shows us the wisdom of others. And experience—often painful and unforgiving—is the lesson that sears itself into your being. So, how do you transform failure from a weight into a weapon of growth? Let it teach you.

EXPLORATION TIME
How Can You Transform Failure Into Growth?

Embrace failure without shame. Stop running from it. Failure is not a reflection of your worth—it is proof you are evolving. Embrace it, not with clenched fists, but with open arms. The pain will come, but so will the growth. Every time you stumble, you step closer to truth.

Learn from the pain. Failure hurts. Sometimes it hits harder than expected. But pain is a messenger, not a verdict. Never bury it—listen. What did it reveal? Some lessons whisper. Some lessons roar. All are here to teach you something you would not have learned otherwise.

Use feedforward instead of feedback. Feedforward shifts your focus from what went wrong to how you can evolve and improve. Instead of carrying the weight of past failures, ask, "What can I do differently next time?" Let the lessons propel you forward.

Celebrate resilience. Acknowledge your ability to rise after every fall. Resilience is not avoiding pain; it is becoming stronger because of it. True resilience means standing tall, even when you have every reason to fall.

Practice self-compassion. Treat yourself with the same kindness you would offer a friend. Consider the Hawaiian practice of Ho'oponopono as a reminder to release guilt and embrace gratitude. Transformation begins with radical self-compassion.

Failure is painful. Disturbing. Humbling. Yet every major transformation in your life has likely been born from it. Resilience is not avoiding pain; it is becoming stronger because of it. True resilience means standing tall, even when you have every reason to fall.

The truth about setbacks is that they make you feel useless. Life will knock you down. Sometimes, it will feel like life is laughing while you struggle to rise. The real enemy? That voice inside—the one whispering you are broken, unworthy, defeated. It is a lie.

Stop labelling yourself a failure. The world profits from making you feel inadequate. Social media glorifies perfection. Yet the truth is, perfection is an illusion. Mistakes are not flaws—they are fingerprints of growth. So, when failure knocks the wind out of you, ask yourself this: Did it break you—or did it reveal a version of you who refuses to quit?

Failure has the power to break you, but in its wake, it also holds the key to refining you— shaping a version of yourself that is stronger, wiser, more resilient, and antifragile.

REFLECTION QUESTIONS
When was the last time you felt failure shake you, and what did it reveal?
How have past failures shaped the way you see yourself today?
What would shift if you embraced failure not as an end, but as a teacher?

Chapter 38: The Subtle Battle of Power vs. Force

"I have the power!" declared He-Man, sword raised high, a symbol of strength echoing across generations.

Yet, in the world of the Sith, power takes a darker form. "The dark side of the Force is a pathway to many abilities some consider to be unnatural," whispered the Sith Lord, his voice laced with manipulation.

Two sides of the same word. Power. But what is it, really? True power transforms. Force, disguised as strength, crushes.

Power and force—two forces that define not just personal experiences but entire generations. Dr. Susan Jeffers and Dr. David Hawkins spoke deeply about these energies. Power is rooted in truth, courage, and compassion. Force thrives on fear, control, and suppression, disguised as strength.

I have known both. And so have you.

As a child, my father would offer me a single finger to hold. Never his whole hand. Not because he withheld care—but because he understood my hands were too small to hold the full weight. That was power. Gentle. Respectful. He gave me the freedom to hold on without overwhelming me.

Force would have crushed my hand. Force would have squeezed tighter, thinking that control was care. But it never was.

My mother showed power in a different way. With her broken English, she stood firm against those who mistreated her. Even when she faced verbal abuse and silence from certain family members, she did not cower. She spoke up, not with force but with courage. She was unafraid to express her truth, even when it was met with resistance. That was power—to hold space for herself without crushing anyone else.

But over the years, the weight of this mistreatment wore her down. She was oppressed, and eventually, she started to believe life was meant to be that way for the younger members of the family—because the elders said so. She got engulfed to the very force she once stood up to, as the pain of repeated suppression convinced her it was unavoidable.

It is highly possible I inherited my rebellious streak from my mother—a rebel with a cause. I have taken many actions she remains angry about to this day. Yet, I know that courageous spark still lingers within her. If it ever rekindles, she will show me immense compassion, as she will realise, I stood up to mistreatment as she did.

Force masquerades as strength. It appears in the teacher who humiliates instead of teaches. The parent who calls it 'protection' while controlling a child's path out of fear. The government that invades in the name of peace. It is the boss who micromanages instead of trusts. It is the voice that yells louder when it feels unheard.

As said in Spider-Man, "With great power comes great responsibility." Yet, when power goes to someone's head, the illusion of invincibility creeps in, transforming strength into toxic force. This is when the person stops guiding and begins to dominate, abuse becoming authoritarian and controlling instead.

And then there is the nonsense around "manifestation." This is where force pretends to be power and gets sold as a magical solution. You have heard it—"Just manifest your desires, and the universe will hand them to you." As if the universe is your servant, waiting to deliver your dreams on a platter. Let us be real—the word "manifestation" has been twisted and abused beyond recognition. It is no longer about growth; it is about control, wrapped up in pretty packaging.

Here is the truth: the universe owes you nothing. You cannot push, pull, or force it to give you what you want. Force demands outcomes—it screams, "Give me what I deserve!" Power does the opposite. Power collaborates. The universe finds it difficult to respond to your ego or your sense of entitlement. It reflects your energy, your truth, and your alignment. Real manifestation is not about shouting commands into the void; it is about working with the energy around you. And yes, the bitter truth many times the answer is still, "No".

The thing is, we are manifesting all the time, but we only celebrate it when it works in our favour. When life hands us what we want, we call it a success. When it cannot, we look for someone or something to blame—karma, bad luck, or the person next door. Meanwhile, an entire industry of manifestation gurus' profits from this lie, convincing us that we can control the universe if we just think positive thoughts. This is manipulation with glitter on top. Manifestation fails because life is more complex than their shallow promises. Karma, deep pain, and unresolved trauma are always in the mix. Let us be honest—no one wants to manifest divorce, poverty, illness, or heartbreak. Yet these things show up in our lives anyway. They are just as much a part of the energy we create as the good things we chase.

And then there is the illusion of being religious, spiritual, or conscious. None of these paths make you immune to the realities of power and force. Being spiritual does not lift you above accountability. Being religious does not give you a moral pass to control others. Consciousness is not about avoiding pain or pretending to be untouchable. If anything, these paths demand more. They demand that you face the hard truths, confront your mess, and live with integrity. True power is not found in sermons, rituals, or declarations. It is found in the relentless labour to live with courage, humility, and truth.

Force grabs and chokes because it is afraid to let go. But power? Power transforms.

Force feels safe when you are broken. It tells you, "Dominate or be dominated." The pain you bury turns into poison—tightening your jaw, raising your voice, and closing your fists. Power asks more of you. Power needs you to let your guard down. It never controls or crushes. Power guides. Power listens. And that is why power is rare—because vulnerability is hard, but control is easy.

When people listen to and follow someone's guidance, they do so out of trust—trusting that the person has their best interests at heart. But far too often, those entrusted with power begin to relish the authority. They lose sight of care and slip into force, controlling rather than guiding.

I have seen and felt power—when a friend sat with me in silence instead of offering advice. When a mentor held space without controlling my choices. When someone believed in me without fixing me. That was power.

EXPLORATION TIME
How Can You Shift from Force to Power?
Identify where you have used force as protection.
Reflect on moments where control felt necessary.
Ask if it was rooted in fear rather than care.

Observe power in practice. Think of situations where you or others guided with patience, trust, and openness rather than control.

Shift your actions. Replace micromanagement with trust. Choose courage over control, even when it feels uncomfortable.

Strengthen emotional awareness. Notice when force emerges as a response to fear. Breathe, pause, and choose power instead.

Ask for guidance. Invite those you lead to share how they feel—does your presence feel empowering or overbearing?

Power liberates. Force suffocates. True power does not need to control. It holds space. It allows. It transforms.

Force crushes. Power liberates. Force demands. Power invites. True power is about giving. It never demands obedience. It asks you to stand in the mirror and say, "I am being wholesome" or "I am being unwholesome." It is not about image. It is about courage—the strength to admit when you have failed, to own your missteps, and to choose a different way.

Force is fragile. It breaks under its own weight. Power is anti-fragile. It adapts. It evolves. It transforms. Power is not the loudest voice. It is not the strongest grip. It is not the last word.

Power is the quiet courage to stand in your truth without needing to crush anyone else to feel whole.

REFLECTION QUESTIONS
Where have you mistaken force for power in your life?
How can you stop controlling and start trusting?
What would shift in your relationships if you led with power instead of fear?

PART VI: Navigating Life's Contradictions

As we move forward from Part V's reflections on money, power, and freedom, it becomes clear that life refuses to fit neatly into categories. For every pursuit of power, there is a lesson in humility. For every moment of freedom, there lies a quiet interdependence we cannot ignore.

Contradictions have been woven into the very fabric of existence for as long as we have searched for meaning. They build us up and break us down, offering moments of clarity and confusion all at once. Love them or resist them, they shape our lives in ways we cannot ignore.

Happiness and pain often arrive hand in hand, just as purpose wrestles with uncertainty and simplicity hides behind complexity. This part is not here to resolve these tensions. It is here to explore them—to sit with the discomfort and reflect on what these contradictions reveal about our humanity.

The chapters ahead will not offer solutions wrapped in certainty but you will certainly find yourself gaining equanimity. They will offer stories—raw, real, and unpolished. You will encounter moments where joy and pain dance together, where clarity emerges only after chaos, and where strength grows quietly in the face of vulnerability.

This section asks you not to fear life's contradictions but to understand them. They are not here to define you. They are here to expand you. The question is not how to avoid them but how to live fully within them.

Welcome to PART VI: Navigating Life's Contradictions. Let us step into this together.

Chapter 39: Happiness Is All We Seek

"If you're happy and you know it, clap your hands." Remember that childhood song? Simple, catchy, and yet profoundly misunderstood. It makes happiness sound like a performance. Clap if you feel it—because if you don't, something must be wrong, right?

And then there's the famous line from Don't Worry, Be Happy. Simple advice, but how many times has it felt like an insult when life was anything but easy?

Alright, let us get real—happiness is not some glittery prize waiting at the end of the rainbow. And you know it. But you have been sold a lie, have you not? The one where happiness gets dangled like a carrot: land that dream job, hit that relationship jackpot, get the ripped abs, and stack your bank account sky-high. Then—only then—you will be happy.

So, you run harder, grind longer, burn yourself out chasing this mythical finish line. And for what? That brief hit of dopamine when you cross something off your list.

Here is the truth no one wants to say out loud:
Happiness is not hiding. It has been there all along—
like a bamboo seed buried so deep inside you that
you forgot how to notice it. Bamboo does not chase
rain. It just grows. Steady. Rooted. Bending when life
storms in but never breaking. Imagine living like that.
Unshakable. Strong.

But let us be honest—nobody teaches you this.
Nobody tells you how to water that seed. They teach
you how to win, how to hustle, how to collect trophies.
But happiness? That seed gets buried under layers of
noise—your past, your fears, your need to prove
yourself.

And life? Life will knock you out many times. Pain will
crash in like an uninvited guest. Loss will sting.
Disappointment will feel unbearable. And yet—
happiness can sit right next to all of it. No, it will not
erase the pain. But it can coexist with it.
That is the contradiction no one talks about—
happiness and pain can hold hands. One does not
need to erase the other. You can feel broken and
whole at the same time. You can ache and still feel

moments of light.

It reminds me of the nursery rhyme: *Row, row, row your boat, gently down the stream. Merrily, merrily, merrily, merrily, life is but a dream.* It is one of the simplest yet most profound lessons about life and happiness. The boat? That is your life. The stream? The flow of existence—sometimes calm, sometimes turbulent. The act of rowing? That is your effort— steady, consistent, but gentle. It is not about fighting the current; it is about flowing with it. And "merrily"? It is not about forced joy. It is about finding lightness even amidst the weight. "Life is but a dream" is a reminder of impermanence—a gentle nudge to cherish each fleeting moment without clinging.

Now here comes the hard part—what about when you cannot even pay your bills? When you are wondering how to keep the lights on or feed your family? Happiness seems like a cruel joke then, right? But here is the uncomfortable truth: happiness is not the absence of problems. It is how you face them without losing yourself. Even in those brutal moments, connection, presence, and gratitude are still possible.

Hard? Yes. Impossible? No.

But what about those individuals who, because of financial hardship—yes, dire hardship—are unable to provide basic essentials for themselves and their loved ones? What about those who find themselves in desperation, turning to drug dealing, prostitution, or even acts of violence? Where does happiness fit into their story? What do they do?

I lack the steps to lift you out of the depths you are in. I lack a blueprint that will erase the desperation or provide the opportunities you deserve. I lack a quick solution for the systems that failed you long before you were even born. What I have is recognition of your reality—a reality most choose to avoid because it feels too uncomfortable to face.

The truth is happiness cannot be imposed or forced. For those in situations where survival itself is a daily battle, happiness is not the answer being sought. It is dignity, equity, compassion, and change. And yet, even within this harsh reality, small acts of humanity—a shared meal, a moment of safety, a fleeting connection—can begin to light the smallest sparks of hope. They are not solutions, but they are reminders that life, even in its rawest form, still holds moments of value.

Perhaps happiness for them begins with creating pathways that lead to dignity—not by sugar-coating the pain, but by acknowledging it. By providing spaces where their voices are heard and their struggles understood. It is never about perfection but about planting seeds of strength and change that will grow with time.

It is never about ignoring the depths of suffering but about finding those flickers of humanity that offer a chance for something more. I have no steps. But together, as a society, perhaps we can start building them.

And happiness is not passive. It is not "think positive thoughts" or slap a smile on your face and call it a day. Real happiness is about creating moments of calm in the chaos. Start small. Sit with yourself, even in discomfort. Journal. Walk without music blasting in your ears. Check in with the parts of yourself you keep shoving aside.

EXPLORATION TIME
How Can You Begin Experiencing True Happiness?

Pause and identify small joys. Acknowledge one simple joy in your day—a quiet moment, a smile, the sun on your face.

Embrace emotional duality. Write down a moment where happiness coexisted with pain. Reflect on how both feelings can exist without cancelling each other out.

Reduce noise. Identify areas where external noise (like social media, people, or places) might be clouding your sense of peace and reduce your exposure.

Create space for stillness. Spend one, three, five minutes or more in silence daily. Let yourself be present without distractions.

Reframe your definition of success. Write your own definition of happiness beyond material achievement.

The Harvard Study of Adult Development, which began in 1938 and is one of the longest-running scientific studies on human well-being, reveals something profoundly simple. The single greatest contributor to long-term happiness is not wealth, fame, or achievements—it is the quality of our relationships. Emotional connection, vulnerability, and trust are the foundations of lasting well-being, far above any external success or perfection.

It is about embracing the contradictions—feeling both the light and the dark. Letting joy and struggle coexist without cancelling each other out. Because the truth is, you do not need perfect circumstances to feel happiness. It is already there. Beneath the noise. Waiting.

Stop buying into the illusion that you need to fix yourself to be happy. You are not broken. You never were. Maybe a bit bruised, sure—but happiness is not about being flawless. It is about showing up fully, imperfections and all.

Happiness is not a finish line. It is the ground you are already standing on—if you stop long enough to feel it.

REFLECTION QUESTIONS
When have you felt happiness without needing external validation?
How does the constant chase for "more" distance you from the happiness already present?
What small step can you take today to stop chasing and start being?

Chapter 40: Pain Is Real, So Is Joy

Life, I am not angry with you (okay, no hiding the truth—yes, I do get angry at times). I am just overwhelmed by the relentless weight of your many questions, especially when they are so direct and raw. You show up without warning, asking things I never thought I would need to answer. And with those questions comes pain. Real. Heavy. Uninvited.

I never imagined living would mean holding this much pain and being compassionate with it. Yet here I am, still standing. Not because the pain has disappeared. Not because I have conquered it. But because something deeper—something unshakable—has kept me moving forward. Like roots beneath a storm, silent but strong.

I have held my pain close, sometimes so close it felt like it was seeping into my bones. I have carried it like an old companion, hoping one day it would grow lighter. I have smiled through it, but not because the weight lessened—because I had no choice but to keep going.

No one teaches you how to hold pain while the world expects you to smile. No one prepares you for how it lingers—unseen by others but loud within you. That smile? Many times, it feels like a mask. Many times, it feels like my lips are hiding truths too heavy to speak.

But here is what they never tell you—pain and joy are not enemies. We have been conditioned to believe that they cannot coexist, that one must be silenced for the other to breathe. But what if they could sit together? What if joy is not what comes after pain, but what rises with it?

Pain carves you open. It strips you raw, exposes your most fragile places. And yet, in that rawness, there is room—room where joy quietly waits. Not loud. Not celebratory. But present. Joy is the breath you finally take after sobbing. Joy is the sun peeking through after a storm. Joy is the friend who whispers, "I see you," when the world feels too heavy.

Much like the deep words of the Hindi song "Kahin Door Jab Din Dhal Jaye"—where the quiet beauty of dusk mingles with the ache of longing—joy does not erase the ache. It lives beside it. The setting sun, tender and melancholic, arrives quietly, much like the moments of joy that pierce through pain without asking for permission. The tears in your eyes, the breath caught in your chest—they do not stop the warmth that rises with them.

And just as in "Kun Faya Kun", where divine surrender transforms suffering into peace, pain softens when we release control. "Kun Faya Kun"—Be, and it is. That letting go, that surrender, does not mean giving up. It means trusting that pain is not the whole story—that there is something greater unfolding, even when it feels impossible to see.

And when I hear the words of "Tere Ishq Nachaya", by Baba Bulleh Shah, I feel the same truth. "Your love has made me dance like mad." This divine joy, even in pain, does not erase the ache but makes it more profound. Pain is no longer a punishment; it becomes a gateway to the deepest expression of being alive. The love, the ache, the surrender—they intertwine until you realise joy was never absent. It was always dancing alongside the pain.

And when I think of courage, I hear the words of Guru Gobind Singh Ji from the sacred Shabad: "Deh Shiva bar mohe eh hai, subh karman te kabh na taron." Grant me the strength, O Lord, to never stray from righteousness. To face pain not with defeat, but with purpose.

"Na daro aar so jab jaye laro, nischay kar apni jeet karon." Let me not fear even when I enter the battlefield but fight with the certainty of victory—not over others, but over my own doubts and despair.

I have fought through the storms, clashing with every shadow, and somewhere along the way, I stopped asking for the storm to end (yes, there are many times I do ask it to stop and leave me alone). Instead, I learned to find my ground while the rain poured. I am no longer waiting for life to be perfect to feel whole. This is tough and rough for me as change and transformation are not linear but all over the place.

EXPLORATION TIME
How Can You Accept Pain Without Losing Joy?

Identify a moment of emotional duality. Think of a time when you felt both pain and joy. Write it down. What did that moment teach you?

Allow both to coexist. Stop suppressing pain to make space for joy. Let both emotions breathe without cancelling each other out.

Stop waiting for perfect healing. Embrace that you can feel whole even while carrying pain.

Create a ritual of release. Listen to music, write a letter to your pain, or express yourself creatively to acknowledge both emotions.

Acknowledge your strength. Reflect on how holding both pain and joy has made you stronger, not weaker.

I once searched for calm waters, believing peace and happiness meant the absence of struggle. But I have learned the truth—happiness is not found in calm. It is forged in chaos. Peace and happiness are never about avoiding the storm; they are about discovering you can stand in the rain, soaked, even when broken.

You never have to erase pain to feel joy. You never have to be healed completely to be whole. Pain and joy—they belong together. They have always coexisted.

Stop waiting for the pain to disappear before you allow yourself to feel joy. Let both be part of your story—because they already are.

REFLECTION QUESTIONS:
When have you experienced moments of joy despite pain?
How do you tend to view pain and joy—separate or connected?
What might change if you allowed both feelings to coexist?

Chapter 41: Simplicity Yet We Overcomplicate Life

There's a poem called "Autobiography in Five Short Chapters" by Portia Nelson. It tells the story of walking down a street and repeatedly falling into the same hole. The first time, you fall in, unaware, lost and helpless. The second time, you see the hole but still fall in. The third time, you fall in again but know it's your fault. The fourth time, you walk around the hole. And finally, in the fifth chapter, you choose a different street entirely.

Simplicity begins when we stop pretending the hole isn't there.

We overcomplicate everything. Life, love, success, happiness—it is as if we have been trained to believe the more tangled it feels, the more valuable it must be. Yes, we have been getting it all wrong.

Look around. Look within. The truth is simplicity has always been the most powerful state. The most honest one. But we run from it. We confuse noise for

meaning. We mask our insecurities with clutter—emotional, mental, physical, spiritual, and materialistic. Layers on layers, hiding the very peace we claim to seek.

And yet, there's a modern phenomenon amplifying this chaos: FOMO—the Fear of Missing Out. It fuels our overcomplication. We scroll through curated feeds of vacations, parties, luxury items, and picture-perfect relationships. We compare, thinking, If I don't have what they have, I'm less. FOMO feeds on insecurity, creating an endless chase to keep up, to prove our worth through possessions, experiences, and appearances. It convinces us that missing out equals falling behind.

Take social media, for instance. It magnifies FOMO by showing us only the highlight reels of others' lives: the extravagant trips, the expensive meals, the idyllic relationships. It's a trap, making us feel like spectators in our own lives. We start believing we must join every event, buy every trending gadget, or share every experience to matter. And in the process, we complicate our lives with things and relationships that don't align with our true selves.

The antidote? JOMO—the Joy of Missing Out. It's the quiet rebellion against this noise. It's the courage to step back and say, I never need to chase this to feel whole. JOMO invites us to find joy in what we have, not in what we lack. It's about choosing the dinner with a close friend over the flashy event. It's about appreciating your well-worn car instead of upgrading to the latest model just because others are. JOMO lets us embrace simplicity, not as deprivation, but as freedom.

The truth is brutal: You are the reason your life feels complicated, yes, it is your karma, deep-seated trauma, conditioning, and much more. Not society. Not your parents. Not your job. You. You cling to the distractions, the attachments, the endless chase for more. And for what? What are you really chasing?

And then there is the wisdom of the Sikh shabad: 'Jiyo main kya maangu, kuchh phir na rahai, har dije naam pyaari'—What more should I ask for? Grant me only Your Name, O Lord. Imagine that—reaching a place where you no longer seek, no longer complicate your existence with endless desires. Just presence. Just being.

But we resist that. We hoard pain. We hold onto expectations. We overthink conversations from years ago. We attach ourselves to things and people like they can fill some void we refuse to face.

Now, you might be thinking—But I need to work. I need to earn. I need to grow. I need to have an opinion and fight for my rights. Isn't that necessary? Yes, it is. But simplicity never means abandoning growth. It means clarifying why you are chasing it. Is your pursuit driven by fear of being mediocre or toxic comparison? Or by a deeper calling to become more of yourself?

EXPLORATION TIME
How Can You Embrace Simplicity and Shift from FOMO to JOMO?

Pause and question the chase. When tempted to buy, attend, or compare, ask: Am I doing this because it matters to me, or because I feel I'll fall behind if I don't?

Celebrate small joys. Shift your focus to the everyday: the sunlight streaming through your window, the joy of a meal you cooked yourself, or a moment of laughter with a loved one.

Declutter your life. Identify material possessions, commitments, or habits that complicate your life. Let go of one thing that no longer serves you.

Find joy in saying no. Practice choosing absence over attendance. Skip the event, the purchase, or the expectation. Feel the freedom in not chasing.

Reclaim relationships. Focus on meaningful connections over superficial ones. Spend time with people who nourish your spirit rather than drain it.

Simplicity is never about giving up. It's about letting go—of the things, beliefs, and patterns that no longer serve you. It's about dismantling the lie that more equals better. Simplicity is asking yourself: Why am I holding onto this pain? Who am I trying to impress? What would happen if I stopped?

And here is the most radical truth of all: You never need to do more to be worthy. You never need to prove anything to anyone. Not your parents. Not society. Not even yourself.

Simplicity is courage, clarity, conviction, and compassion. The courage to strip it all down until you are left with only what matters: love, connection, truth. The clarity to see through distractions, the conviction to stay true to yourself, and the compassion to release what no longer serves you.

REFLECTION QUESTIONS:
What unnecessary complexities have you added to your life out of fear or ego?

How has FOMO driven your decisions, and how could JOMO offer relief?

What would simplicity look like for you, not as an idea, but as a daily practice?

MY CREED: TO DO THE BEST I CAN, DESPITE THE ODDS

Chapter 42: Find Joy in the Smallest Things

We have made joy so damn complicated. We act as if it's this grand, elusive treasure—reserved for those who've earned it, as if happiness is some exclusive reward handed out after ticking all of society's arbitrary boxes: wealth, success, validation, perfection. And guess what? That chase never ends.

But joy? Real joy? It was never hiding at the finish line. It was never something you had to earn. Joy has always been here—in the quiet moments you've been too busy to notice. The sunlight warming your skin. The cup of tea savoured without distraction. The sound of your own breathing—simple, unremarkable, and yet profoundly alive.

And still, we resist simplicity. Why? Because simplicity strips away the noise we cling to. It forces us to face what we've been running from: the discomfort, the void, the fear that maybe—just maybe—all this striving was never necessary. So, we overcomplicate everything. We convince ourselves we need more.

More accomplishments. More admiration. More proof that we are enough.

∞

Mary Oliver's The Summer Day holds a mirror to this complexity. Through her quiet reverence for the present, she reminds us that life's magic lies not in some grand pursuit, but in the art of noticing. Her words, "What is it you plan to do with your one wild and precious life?" cut to the heart of overcomplication. Life's value is not in endless striving but in mindful appreciation of the ordinary.

Similarly, Bulla Ki Jaana Main Kaun by Bulleh Shah resonates with the simplicity we seem to fear. It peels away labels, constructs, and the roles we attach ourselves to, inviting us to see life's core essence: being. The refrain—"Bulla! ki jaana main kaun" (Bulleh, to me, I am not known)—echoes the human struggle with self-created complexities, reminding us that joy and peace lie in shedding, not adding.

And if you think joy can only exist when life is perfect, consider Nelson Mandela, the anti-apartheid revolutionary and former President of South Africa.

Stripped of control. Stripped of freedom. Yet even behind bars, he chose inner freedom. He found simplicity, not by surrendering to defeat but by focusing on what truly mattered—love, dignity, truth. Joy was never about his circumstances. It was about his clarity. His conviction. His refusal to let pain own him.

Here's the uncomfortable truth: we complicate joy because simplicity terrifies us. It threatens the very stories we've been fed since childhood—the idea that fitting in, conforming, and achieving makes us worthy. We fear the judgment of stepping outside the expected. What will people think if you stop chasing, stop achieving, stop proving? So, we keep performing, keep pleasing, keep adding layers of noise to avoid the discomfort of being seen for who we really are.

The world has conditioned you to seek approval, to stay in line, to match the pace of those around you. But that cycle never ends. Simplicity challenges this, stripping away those layers of expectation, asking you to stop performing and just be. And yes, that's terrifying. But it's also where real freedom begins. We're scared that if we stop chasing, we'll have to confront the void. The pain. The truth we keep numbing with busyness and noise.

EXPLORATION TIME

So how do you stop missing joy?

Stop overthinking happiness. Joy doesn't need to be complex. It lives in the moments you keep dismissing—like the way your breath feels after a deep sigh.

Notice the overlooked. Joy shows up in the tiny spaces—the steam rising from your morning coffee, the sound of rain tapping on your window.

Let go of the 'big picture.' Stop waiting for some massive, life-altering event to feel joy. Start where you are.

Be present with your senses. Feel the warmth of your skin under sunlight. Taste your food. Hear

your breath. Joy speaks through presence, not perfection.
Stop making it conditional. You never need to have your life figured out to feel joy. It's here already. In the cracks. In the now.

And yet, modern life has turned simplicity into a luxury. The world has taken minimalism, silence, and basic comforts—then wrapped them in exclusivity, branding them as status symbols.

Think about it: five-star retreats promising 'digital detox' for thousands of dollars just to take your phone away. Luxury brands selling 'simple' white shirts for ridiculous prices because they've sold the lie that less equals status. A minimalist hotel room with no clutter, no distractions—just a mountain view—and an absurd nightly rate.

Simplicity isn't supposed to be commodified. But we've allowed the world to profit off of our need for clarity and peace. Simplicity was never about exclusivity. It's not reserved for the wealthy. It's available in the ordinary, the unpolished moments—

the way your heartbeat slows in the quiet, the unexpected kindness of a stranger, the sound of your own breath reminding you you're alive.

Joy never asks for conditions. It asks for presence. It asks you to stop waiting, stop performing, stop apologising for being where you are. Joy is about showing up to the messy, unfiltered reality of your life—without needing it to be perfect first.

Joy is not a perfectly packaged experience. It is raw, imperfect, and deeply personal. It is the quiet defiance of choosing to breathe deeply when the world tells you to keep running. It is finding peace in a single ordinary moment, not because life is flawless, but because you finally allowed yourself to be here, fully present.

Joy is not reserved for perfection. It exists in the raw, unfiltered moments. The ones where you stop chasing, stop apologising, and finally allow yourself to feel alive—just as you are, right here, right now.

REFLECTION QUESTIONS

What unnecessary complexities have you added to your life out of fear or ego?

How would your life change if you let go of needing to control everything?

What would simplicity look like for you, not as an idea, but as a daily practice?

Chapter 43: Time for Exploration, No Need For Purpose or Passion

Life purpose. Passion. Callings. These ideas have been sold to you as if they are the only way to live a life that matters. The self-help world has pushed it relentlessly: "Find your why! Discover your purpose! Chase your passion!" But what if it is all just another illusion?

Yes, it sounds inspiring. I believed it too. I chased it for years, thinking my sense of purpose and passion would lead me to success, fulfilment, that magical life where everything just fits perfectly. But reality? My sense of purpose and passion never guaranteed success. They did not come with a map. They did not prevent failure, heartbreak, or moments of absolute chaos.

And then, I noticed something uncomfortable. I saw people who had no grand sense of purpose. No intense drive. People who were not chasing some profound "why." And guess what? They were happier than most. They were living fully, content, engaged with the simple, small joys life offered—without trying to make it all a performance.

Here is the hard truth no one wants to admit: The whole "find your purpose" obsession has become a business, a fashion and fad statement. It has been twisted into another hustle—a cycle convincing you that unless you are pursuing some divine, all-consuming mission, you are somehow failing at life.

Purpose and passion have become buzzwords and they are often misunderstood. Passion is a great drive that can fuel you, but when forced, it becomes a burden. Purpose is wonderful as it can give you direction and focus, especially when you feel lost. Both purpose and passion give you some kind of will to live and can provide clarity, but when rigid, they trap you.

Exploration? Now that—that is freedom. Exploration is experiencing life without attachment. No agenda. No need to prove yourself. Exploration makes space for creativity, learning, innovation, and growth—without the obsession of getting it right.

Let me be clear: Having personal drive (passion) and direction (purpose) can be extremely powerful. They can spark something beautiful, but only when they are organic—not when you are forcing them like some checklist item, some kind of competition, some kind of "look at me, world" or "I need to do this because everyone else is doing it."

When you explore—truly explore—you drop the pressure. You stop measuring yourself. You stop obsessing over results and outcomes. Suddenly, life becomes about being present, learning, feeling, discovering. You stop saying, "I have no direction, no personal drive," as if you are broken. Because you are whole.

Some of the happiest people I have met have zero personal drive and no purpose. No five, ten, or twenty-year plan or burning obsession to leave a legacy. They live in the moments. They cook meals with love. They find joy in their work. They laugh. They sit under the sun without needing it to mean anything. And they are whole.

Exploration is what frees you. When you explore, you embrace the unknown with curiosity, not fear. Expectation drops. Letting go becomes easier because you are not clinging to what you think should happen.

Exploration says: "Let us see what this experience brings."
Purpose says: "This must be meaningful."
Passion says: "Feel this deeply—it must define you."
Exploration whispers: "Give it a go. Just be here."
Purpose insists: "If you are not successful, you are failing."
Passion demands: "You must feel on fire all the time, or it is not real."

But what if you are not broken for not knowing? What if not knowing is part of the beauty?

EXPLORATION TIME
What can you do to explore life without the pressure of defining yourself?

Engage in a new experience this week without any expectation of success or mastery.
Reflect on moments when you felt joy without needing a deeper reason—what made them feel so light?

Release the need for labels in your current pursuits—drop the question of whether it fits your "purpose."

Notice where you are forcing passion—what happens when you let yourself simply be present?

Embrace curiosity as a way of life, asking yourself, "What can I learn from this moment without needing to control it?" You never need a profound calling to be worthy of a full life. And you certainly never need to buy into the hustle of "find your why." That pressure is a lie.

So, what if you just explored? No labels. No pressure. Just you, showing up for life, present and open. And if you are not ready for that yet? Fine. Flow. Breathe. Be mindful. Be wholesome.

Life will keep moving, with or without your permission, passion, or purpose.

REFLECTION QUESTIONS
When did you last feel pressured to define your life by purpose or personal drive?
How might your life feel different if you embraced exploration instead?
What simple moments have brought you joy without needing a deeper meaning?

Chapter 45: The Strength to Rise When You Want to Quit

There comes a point where you break. Not crack—break. The weight becomes so unbearable, the voice inside whispers, "Enough. Stop. You have given all you can." And you believe it because the exhaustion feels endless, and the fight feels unwinnable.

But strength? It is not the absence of breaking. It is not being untouched by pain. Strength is found in the moments after—the silent choice to rise, even when you have every reason to stay down.

You might think rising requires some magical burst of courage. It does not. It is often quieter than that. Rising sometimes looks like taking a single breath after the breakdown. It is the hand that grips the edge of the bed when the weight feels too heavy. It is the whisper—not today—even when you are still drowning.

Billy Ocean's words echo here: "When the going gets tough, the tough get going." It sounds motivational on the surface, but those words only come alive when you are gasping for air, when the world feels unforgiving. And yet, there is something in them— something raw. A truth beneath the cliché.

True toughness—the kind that keeps you standing when you want to quit—is not about pushing harder, pretending the pain does not exist, or forcing yourself to ignore the cracks. It is about resilience. And resilience is not born from brute force but from courage, clarity, conviction, and compassion.

Courage is not the absence of fear but the decision to face it anyway. The breath you take before standing back up. The choice to try again, even when the odds mock you. Courage whispers, "I may not win today, and yes, I might break, but I will find a way to move on. Yes, I might give up, yet I will find a way to rise."

Clarity is a bright, shining light that shows you everything. When everything is chaotic, and the noise of failure screams in your head, clarity becomes your anchor, even if it's only a flicker of light. It is not about controlling everything but about creating focus amidst the noise. It is the reminder that even in pain, there is still life. That the next step matters, even if it feels small. Clarity allows you to strip away the noise and focus on what truly matters—What can I focus on right now?

Conviction is not believing; it goes beyond it. It is the knowing that you are not done yet. Not because you feel strong, but because you learn with time this moment never will define you. Conviction is not arrogance—it is a leap of faith, deep within, that this struggle is not the end of your story. It is holding faith, even when it feels ridiculous.

Compassion towards yourself is not selfishness. The world romanticises grit but forgets the power of kindness and care—the strength it takes to be gentle with yourself when everything feels impossible. Compassion says, "You are allowed to feel this pain. But it never will own you."

In 2020, when the world shut down, billions felt powerless. Lives were upended. Dreams were crushed. And yet, people kept rising. Not because they were fearless, but because they found the courage to face the unknown, the clarity to adapt, the conviction to keep moving, and the compassion to forgive themselves for feeling broken.

It is not about fighting harder. It is about being anti-fragile—allowing pain to shape you, not shatter you. And even if it shatters, remember kintsugi—the Japanese art of mending broken pottery with gold, turning the cracks into a part of its beauty, not a flaw. Nassim Nicholas Taleb described anti-fragility as the ability not just to withstand stress but to grow from it. Resilience does not mean being untouched by pain. It means being shaped by it, becoming stronger not in spite of it but because of it.

This struggle is not unique to me or any single individual. We all face moments where life feels unbearably heavy. Some have the fortune of a guiding hand—someone or something that teaches them to regulate these storms, to see beyond the chaos, and not be paralysed by it. But even with guidance, life will throw multiple curveballs again and again. The storms will return. Yet each time they do, the darkness loses its grip, the weight lessens, and the lessons deepen.

Let me also share about my former in-laws. When you meet them, it seems like they have no problems, no worries in the world. But beneath that calm, joyful surface, they have faced immense adversities. Yes, they get upset. Yes, they feel frustration. But somehow, they find the courage, clarity, conviction and compassion to rise again.

Then there are my close friends. From the outside, it may seem their lives are smooth sailing. But they too have weathered storms—personal struggles, troubles the world rarely sees. They rise, not with the glamour of a phoenix emerging from the ashes, but in quiet strength. Sometimes fast, sometimes slow. But always, they rise. They have learned to fail and get back up, while the world only sees their grace.

So, how do we rise?

We rise by remembering that strength is not about perfection. It is about taking the next breath, the next step, no matter how small. It is about choosing, again and again, to keep going. And as we learn from each event, the fear, the pain, the paralysis loses their power.

We rise by letting go of the idea that strength means never breaking. It means allowing yourself to feel, to fall apart if necessary, and still choosing to rebuild.

We rise by releasing the burdens we have clutched for too long—the guilt, the pain, the self-doubt—and recognising that we do not have to carry them alone. Life is already moving forward, already holding us. Trust that process.

We rise by focusing on the smallest next step. Not the entire journey. Just one step—one breath, one choice, one moment of courage.

We rise by leaning on courage, clarity, conviction, and compassion—not as abstract concepts but as the anchors that keep us steady. Courage to face discomfort without turning away. Clarity to focus on what truly matters, not control everything. Conviction to know you are not defined by this struggle. Compassion to be gentle with yourself when you stumble.

And finally, we rise by understanding that growth is rarely graceful. Sometimes you rise in pieces, breath by breath. Sometimes, like kintsugi, you rise by embracing the cracks and making them part of your strength.

EXPLORATION TIME
How to rise when you want to or have quit?

What is one small wholesome step you could take today, no matter how overwhelmed or defeated you feel, to begin rising from your current challenge, pain, struggle or suffering?

Write down one or more emotional weight you are carrying—guilt, fear, or shame. Acknowledge it without judgment.

Take one small action today, like calling a friend or stepping outside, no matter how insignificant it feels.

Choose a mantra like "This is not the end of my story" and repeat it when overwhelmed.

Use a simple breathing exercise to ground yourself in moments of panic—inhale for four counts, hold for four, exhale for six.

Reflect on a time you felt broken but managed to find growth. How did the experience shape you into who you are today?

Rising is not about perfection; it is about strength no matter how microscopic it is. Strength never demands we be fearless. It only asks us to do our best even when we think and feel it is our worst. To breathe. To rise, in whatever small way we can.

So, if you find yourself there—at the edge, exhausted, unable to go on, giving up—remember this: You never have to feel strong to be strong. You never need to have all the answers. You only need to take the next breath. And then the next.

∞

Because that is what strength looks like—rising, even when you want to quit or have quit. And maybe, just maybe, one breath at a time—you will discover you are stronger than you ever imagined.

Rising is rarely glamorous. It is often slow, messy, and deeply personal. There will be days when it feels like you are taking one step forward and ten steps back. But even then, every step matters. Every breath matters. Every act of courage, clarity, conviction, and compassion becomes a building block for your strength.

We rise by accepting the mess. To trust that life is moving forward even when we feel stuck. To embrace the cracks that tell the story of how we became unbreakable.

Strength says fall. It also says to rise, breath by breath, even when it feels impossible and extremely slow —because each breath you take

brings you closer to discovering the unbreakable spirit within you.

REFLECTION QUESTIONS
What emotional burdens are you still holding onto that you can begin to release?
How can you practice rising up in small, manageable steps during difficult times?
Who or what has been a guiding hand for you during challenging moments, and how can you offer that support to others?

Chapter 46. When the World Feels Against You

When the world feels against you, it starts with a whisper. An idea, a belief so subtle it feels like truth: "They are against me."

And from that belief, chaos unfolds. Entire lives, entire histories have been shaped—no, scarred—by this notion. Wars ignited. Families torn apart. Bloodshed, killing and violence. Nations shattered. All because of the unexamined unwholesome belief that someone else is the enemy.

Look closely at the roots of war. Strip away the political theatre, the grand speeches, the flags waving high. At its core lies one simple yet devastating illusion: "They are against us. We must defend. We must strike." Whether fuelled by nationalism, power hunger, or the illusion of superiority, the battle is rarely about truth—it is about belief. A belief that someone must be opposed, resisted, conquered, erased.

Racism? Prejudice? Strip those down too, and you will find the same poison. "They are not like us. They are a threat to us." But who decided that? Who created the invisible walls between skin colours, cultures, faiths? Who whispered that difference was dangerous instead of beautiful?

But let us be clear: This is not about blaming yourself for the harm others inflict. The injustice, the cruelty, the abuse—these are real. And they are not your fault. A child cannot be blamed for the cruelty of an adult. A victim of discrimination does not manifest their own pain. Harmful actions are the responsibility of those who choose them. This is not about letting perpetrators off the hook. It is about recognising the poison of blame—how it seeps into your soul and tells you, "This is who you are now."

Take the example of Dr. Martin Luther King Jr. and Malcolm X—two powerful voices against racial injustice. Dr. King chose non-violence, believing that compassion and peaceful resistance could break the cycle of hate. Malcolm X, in his early years, advocated for self-defense and confronting oppression with force. Both were shaped by personal experiences of injustice and systemic racism, recognising the need to challenge the injustices they faced—not out of a belief that the world was entirely against them, but from a place of seeking justice and equity.

What about the survivors who do not make the history books? A survivor of sexual abuse might stay in toxic relationships, not because they lack strength, but because their self-worth has been systematically destroyed. Or someone who has lived in poverty for decades might take desperate measures to escape it, believing that dignity has a price tag.

These stories are not about glorifying pain. They are about understanding the wreckage that the belief, "The world is against me," leaves behind. It creates prisons—prisons of distrust, fear, and self-destruction. And it tells you that escape is impossible.

EXPLORATION TIME
So, What If the World Really Is Against You?

Acknowledge the pain. The harm done to you is not a reflection of your worth. Recognise the pain but refuse to let it define you.

Set shields. You can hold compassion for others without allowing harmful behaviour to continue. Draw clear lines where necessary.

Seek support. You never have to carry the burden alone. Lean on those who uplift you—whether it is friends, community, or professional help.

Focus on what is wholesome. The injustice feels overwhelming. Anchor yourself in small actions within your power—your response, your healing, your growth.

Turn pain into exploration. Use your experiences to build empathy, support others, and become a voice for positive change.

The world may feel against you, and there are times it truly is. But strength, peace, and meaning can emerge from equanimity—the choice to respond without being consumed by the storm.

∞

When the world feels against you, it tries to take pieces of you. It whispers, "This is all you will ever know. This is who you are." And slowly, you begin to believe it. You let the narrative of pain, anger, and injustice seep into your identity. You let it shape the way you see others and the way you see yourself. But here is the truth they never tell you: You never have to stay in the prison they built for you. You can defy that story. You can write your own.

This is not about erasing the pain or pretending the harm never happened. It is about refusing to let it own you. The world may feel against you, but it never has to define you. It does not have to trap you in its lies.

This is where the concept of Chardi Kala becomes revolutionary. In Sikh philosophy, Chardi Kala is the state of relentless high spirits, undying optimism, and unwavering positivity in the face of life's hardships. It is not the absence of suffering—it is the refusal to let suffering define you. Chardi Kala does not deny pain, but it insists that pain is not the end of the story.

Imagine this: the world may press against you, injustices may pile up, and you may feel the sting of betrayal, loss, and cruelty. Yet Chardi Kala reminds you that even amidst this storm, you can hold your spirit high. Not out of naivety, but out of courage. Not because the pain is fair, but because you refuse to bow to its weight.

It is a declaration of defiance—against despair, against hopelessness, against the lies that tell you your worth is tied to the world's cruelty. Chardi Kala says, "I am more than this. My spirit is more than this. My life will not be measured by the harm inflicted upon me but by the strength with which I rise."

Chardi Kala transforms your response to injustice. It becomes an act of rebellion against everything that tries to break you. It allows you to say: You may take my comfort, my certainty, even my peace for a time. But you will not take my spirit.

Even when the world feels against you, even when the pain is real and unrelenting, Chardi Kala offers a way to rise—not in spite of the struggle but through it. It is the audacity to hold your head high, to remain steadfast, and to believe in your own boundless capacity for freedom.

You can rise—not because the world becomes fair, but because you are free. Free of the narratives that keep you small. Free of the belief that you are powerless.

REFLECTION QUESTIONS
Have you ever felt the world was against you?
How did it shape your actions and beliefs?
What strategies have helped you regain strength during difficult times?
How can you create shields while still practising empathy and compassion?

Chapter 47: Yes! Life Will Never Be Black and White

Life is not black and white. It never has been. Yet, we are conditioned to think in binaries—right and wrong, good and bad, success and failure. But reality? Reality is far messier. It flows, bends, and blurs the edges of what we think we know. It sometimes is grey and other times colourful.

From the moment we are born, we are handed stories. Stories that tell us who we should be, how to think, what to fear. We are taught not to lie, yet we grow up surrounded by half-truths, contradictions, and comfortable illusions. Pain is bad. Pleasure is good. But is it that simple?

Pleasure, when unchecked, can spiral into indulgence—obsession with carnal desires, materialism, and the endless chase for more. Pain, on the other hand, can trap us in victimhood, becoming an excuse for stagnation even when life offers moments of beauty. Neither extreme tells the whole story.

At our core, we all carry seeds—seeds of both the wholesome and unwholesome. Darkness and light. What we water shapes who we become. Some seeds were planted by upbringing, beliefs, trauma, and conditioning—others by personal experience and choice. Yet, as life unfolds, we begin to realise not all seeds need nurturing. Some must wither for us to grow.

It is easy to cling to absolutes—to crave a world where clarity reigns, where every decision fits into neat categories. But life has taught me that true wisdom lies in dissolving those illusions. To strip away the labels—race, gender, culture, belief systems, even spirituality—and ask, What remains?

What remains is being. Raw. Vulnerable. Unlabelled. Beyond the need to prove or justify.

The Japanese concept of Shoshin—the beginner's mind—teaches us that no matter how much we think we know, life will humble us. True wisdom is not intellectual. It is felt. Experienced. Lived. And when you hold life without the need to control it, you begin to see that contradictions are not conflicts—they are complementary forces, working together.

Yin-Yang. Shiva-Shakti. Forces of creation and destruction, light and shadow, feminine and masculine—all coexisting, not cancelling each other out but completing one another. Yet, understanding this concept intellectually is different from living it. Words can describe balance, but they cannot make you feel it.

This truth is often misinterpreted as numbness. But it is not detachment. It is the quiet power of mind flow—moving with life, not against it. It is being flexible, adaptable, yet rooted in respect, integrity, and compassion. It is about letting go of the need to define everything as either right or wrong and instead choosing to listen deeply.

Deep listening reduces the noise of preconceived ideas. It quiets the mind long enough to hear what lies beneath—to hold space for truths that exist beyond judgment. Yet, this practice does not mean perfection. I, too, get provoked. I am no saint. But what has helped me shift is the simple question: What would the wisest person say to me?

∞

Sometimes, the answer is silence. Sometimes, it is breathing. Other times, it is the teachings passed down from mentors like Dr. Segu Ramesh, who taught me the solution exercise—a tool that grounds me when the mind spirals. These tools have not made me immune to pain but have allowed me to move through it with greater ease, without needing to dramatise or suppress it.

And yes, it can be frustrating. Knowing deeply yet struggling to explain. Feeling the weight of contradictions without the words to convey them. But as Thich Nhat Hanh so beautifully taught, true compassion arises not from understanding but from being present—from standing in the discomfort without needing to solve or label it.

Many mistake calmness for weakness. They see restraint as a lack of strength. But real strength is quiet. It does not need theatrics or validation. It requires no drama.

This path is not easy. I still fail. Yet, the progress is undeniable. Each time I choose to breathe rather than react, listen rather than argue, and reflect rather than blame, I reclaim a little more of my power.

Life is not about eliminating contradictions. It is about holding space for them. Letting pain and joy, shadow and light, strength and vulnerability coexist. Because that is where true growth lies—not in avoiding discomfort but in learning to stay present within it.

Exploration Time
What does holding space for contradictions look like in your life right now?

Spend five minutes each day in silence, observing your thoughts without judgment. Notice the contradictions within your mind and hold them with compassion.

Write about a situation where you experienced both joy and pain. Reflect on how these emotions coexisted and what they taught you.

Use "The Solution" taught by Dr. Segu Ramesh. When your mind spirals into extremes, pause and ask yourself, What is one small action I can take right now to restore balance?

Read or learn about a perspective that challenges your current beliefs. Sit with the discomfort it brings and notice how it shifts your understanding.

The next time you feel provoked, take three deep breaths and ask yourself, What would the wisest version of me do right now? Act from that place.

The beauty of life's grey areas is their ability to challenge what you think you know. They pull you out of certainty, forcing you to sit with the discomfort of not knowing. And yet, this discomfort is where life truly begins—not in the clear-cut answers, but in the spaces where opposites meet and transform.

When you embrace contradictions, you are no longer trapped by the need to control. You let go of the exhausting battle to label every experience as right or wrong, good or bad. Instead, you learn to hold life gently, allowing it to show you what lies beyond the surface. You begin to see the richness in the in-between spaces—the quiet truths that cannot be captured by extremes.

Think of the tension between pain and joy, chaos and peace, shadow and light. It is not a weakness to feel both. It is a testament to your depth, your capacity to live fully. Strength is not about eliminating discomfort; it is about becoming the container that holds it all—the heartbreak and the laughter, the uncertainty and the clarity.

This is not about fixing the contradictions but learning to breathe within them. It is about understanding that your worth is not tied to solving every paradox but to being present with them. Because when you stop wrestling with the messiness of life, you discover something extraordinary: the mess is what makes it beautiful.

You are not here to choose one side of life's spectrum. You are here to embody the whole—the joy, the pain, the confusion, the stillness. It is this fullness that makes you human. It is this fullness that sets you free.

The grey areas of life are where wisdom, compassion, and true self-awareness reside. It is in these spaces of uncertainty that you discover the courage to stay open, the strength to remain present, and the clarity to see beauty in life's messiness.

REFLECTION QUESTIONS

What beliefs or experiences have shaped your view of life as black and white?

How can you practice holding space for both pain and joy in your life?

What tools help you stay present when facing life's contradictions?

Chapter 48: You Are Not Broken, You Are Becoming

You were never broken. You are not broken. Stop believing the lie that you are broken.

The cracks you feel, the ache you carry, the moments when life leaves you breathless with disappointment—none of it means you are shattered. None of it means you need fixing.

Yet the world loves selling you this illusion. It whispers through self-help gurus and glossy motivational quotes: "Heal yourself. Fix yourself. Become whole again." As if you were ever incomplete. As if the pain is a problem, not part of the process.

You are not broken. You are becoming.

Your struggles? Your scars? They are not stains. They are your gold seams. The reminders that you have lived, that you have felt deeply, that you have risen again even when the weight seemed unbearable.

But the world does not make space for becoming. It demands perfection. It sells you curated lives, filtered truths, highlight reels where everyone seems whole, thriving, untouched by failure. So, when you fall apart—when the grief lingers, when the fear grips, when the past resurfaces—you feel defective. As if your cracks make you unworthy of love, success, or peace.

Here is the truth no one tells you: The process of becoming is messy. Uncomfortable. Raw. Healing never moves in a straight line. Some days, you will feel powerful, expansive, unstoppable. And other days, you will wonder if you have made any progress at all.

And that is okay.

The pain you feel is not proof of brokenness. It is proof of growth. It is your heart stretching wider. Your spirit expanding. The discomfort of outgrowing versions of yourself that no longer fit. Becoming is uncomfortable because it demands truth. It asks you to sit with the parts of yourself you have hidden. The parts you were told were 'too much' or 'not enough.'

Becoming means unlearning the lies you were fed: that vulnerability equals weakness, that pain makes you flawed, that mistakes define you. No. Your pain reveals where you care deeply. Your mistakes teach you where you are growing. Your vulnerability? That is courage in its purest form.

You are not broken for feeling lost. You are not broken for grieving what you once were. You are not broken for needing time, space, or stillness.

Look at the caterpillar. When it cocoons, it does not merely grow wings and emerge. It dissolves completely—liquefies—before reassembling itself. It becomes unrecognisable before it flies. And so do you.

So, when you feel like you are falling apart, remember you are not broken. You are unbecoming what no longer serves you. You are softening the old stories.

Shedding the skin of who you were told to be, so you can step fully into who you are meant to become.

∞

You do not need to be fixed. You need to be witnessed. Held. Reminded that your cracks are not flaws but doorways. They let the light in.

The beauty of becoming is that there is no finish line. No final version where you have it all together. Growth is not linear. Healing is not a checklist. You will rise. You will stumble. And you will rise again.

I have sensed this myself—like I am only touching the surface of deeper truths yet unexplored. There is a thick layer still between what I know and the depth I have yet to experience. I have not fully dived in, and that is okay. Becoming is not about reaching some profound depth but honouring where you are, right now, with honesty.

EXPLORATION TIME
What would it look like to honour your becoming instead of fearing it?

*Write down moments when you felt "broken."
Reflect on how they shaped you, stretched you,
and made you grow.*

*Next time you feel discomfort, pause and ask
yourself, What is this teaching me? What part of
me is being stretched right now?*

*At the end of each day, note one small way you
moved closer to growth—whether it was resting,
speaking your truth, or simply feeling your
emotions fully.*

*Practise being present with where you are.
Meditate on this thought: I am enough, even as I
am becoming.*

*Share your process with a trusted friend, mentor,
or journal. Let someone or something witness
your becoming without judgment.*

The process of becoming will always demand more
than you think you can give. It will stretch you, shake
you, and unearth parts of yourself you thought were

long buried. But within that discomfort is a quiet power—a reminder that every crack, every ache, every messy moment is shaping you into something extraordinary.

Becoming is not about finding the perfect version of yourself. It is about learning to love the process—the dissolving, the reassembling, the emerging. It is about honouring your growth, not despite its messiness but because of it.

You are not here to prove your worth. You are here to live your life. Every scar, every stumble, every stretch is part of that story. And the beauty of becoming? It does not ask you to be finished. It asks you to be present.

The goal was never to be perfect. It was always to be real. Whole. Human. You are not broken. You are becoming. And becoming? It is beautiful.

REFLECTION QUESTIONS
What parts of yourself have you been hiding, believing they make you broken?

How have your struggles shaped the person you are becoming?

What would change if you embraced your imperfections as part of your strength?

Chapter 49. The Courage to Walk Your Own Path

There is something poetic about standing tall even after massive errors, colossal missteps, and the kind of messiness that leaves scars you feel in your bones. These are not polished stories. They are raw, real, and unapologetically living without seeking fame or approval. They have made massive errors, colossal missteps, and the kind of messiness that leaves scars you feel in your bones. Yet, they stand tall— sometimes out of arrogance, but mostly out of rawness, compassion, and a giving nature that refused to let life harden them.

One defied expectations early. They walked away from the security of a stable career not out of rebellion, but because the script never fit. They made massive errors along the way—trusting the wrong people, believing promises that were never kept. Yet, they stand tall. Not polished. Not perfect. But raw and unshaken in their giving nature. Because their mistakes? They never defined them. They refined them.

Another stayed in relationships that dimmed their light, in situations that shrank their voice. And when they finally chose to walk away, it was not glamorous. It was chaotic. Painful. But they chose themselves—slowly, quietly, without seeking applause. Now, when others tell them they have become "too strong," they smile. Because they cannot see the nights, they cried themselves whole. They cannot see the strength it took to unlearn the idea that shrinking themselves made them lovable.

And then there is the one who fought battles invisible to the world. Addiction, self-doubt, spirals of anger that nearly consumed them. Their rise was not loud. It was slow. Unsteady. But they chose to rise anyway. Today, they give—openly, generously—because they know what it feels like to have nothing left but the raw choice to keep breathing.

Then there is the story of someone who remains oppressed, as if they have been forcefully brainwashed into submission. They have no light left. No flicker of defiance. Only the weight of conformity pressing harder each day. Their courage is not in the defiance they cannot find but in the quiet survival they embody every single day.

And about that what many say— "The mind is everything. You become what you think about." Slam it. Drown it. Kill it. It is absolute bullshit. Life does not bend to motivational soundbites. The mind matters, yes, but it is not everything. You cannot think your way out of generational pain or systemic oppression. Oversimplified slogans will never be the answer.

True courage lies in acknowledging that the mind, while powerful, does not erase the weight of reality. It cannot undo the scars of trauma or the burden of societal expectations. Courage is not found in catchy phrases but in the raw, unfiltered moments of choosing to rise anyway.

Because life is not black and white. Strength is not a mindset. Strength is raw. It is standing tall even when you have every reason to collapse. It is refusing to be defined by mistakes. It is saying, "I am not broken. I am becoming."

EXPLORATION TIME
What does walking your own path look like for you, and where have you been hesitating to take the first step?

Spend 10 minutes in quiet reflection or journaling, asking yourself: What truly is important to me, beyond what others expect of me?

Write down one desire or direction that keeps resurfacing, even if it scares you.

Choose one area of your life where you've been seeking validation and consciously let go. For example, deciding without consulting anyone else's opinion.

Reflect on a recent mistake and reframe it as a lesson. Ask: What did this teach me about myself, my values, or my growth?

Write down three common societal or generational beliefs you've internalised (e.g., "Success means financial wealth," "Perfection equals strength"). Next to each one, write your truth.

Practise sitting with the unknown by choosing one decision you've been avoiding. Break it into smaller steps and take the first one today.

Identify one belief or habit you've inherited but no longer serves you. Begin unlearning it by replacing it with an action aligned with your values.
Stand Tall in Isolation:

Spend a day making choices based purely on your intuition, without explaining or justifying yourself to anyone.

Create a personal definition of success based on your values. Ask yourself: What does a fulfilled life look like for me, not for others?

To have the courage to walk your own path means embracing discomfort, facing your fears, and standing firm in your truth (not arrogance) even when the world questions you.

Walking your own path does not mean the road will be smooth. It will be riddled with uncertainty, failure, and moments of doubt. But within those moments lies the quiet power of self-discovery—the truth that courage is not found in applause or approval but in the raw act of choosing yourself.

This path is not about arrogance or rebellion. It is about authenticity. It is about standing tall in the messiness of your humanity and saying, "This is who I am, and I am enough."

Taking the courage to walk your own path will not guarantee you success or appreciation. It will not shield you from failure or misunderstanding. But it will be the truest expression of your strength and authenticity.

Even when you stand alone, misunderstood and uncelebrated, to walk your own path is proof of a courage so rare it needs no audience.

REFLECTION QUESTIONS

When was the last time you stood tall despite making mistakes?

How much of your life has been shaped by societal expectations rather than your truth?

What would shift if you stopped believing you need to be perfect to be strong?

Chapter 50: In the End, Do Your Best—That's Enough

There is a truth you have been avoiding. Or shall I say, we all have been conditioned and programmed to avoid? A truth so simple, yet so confronting, that the world keeps burying it beneath endless noise.

You were never meant to be perfect. You were meant to be human.

This obsession with perfection—where did it come from? Was it the teachers who praised the A's but punished the effort? Was it the media feeds filled with curated lives, flawless bodies, highlight reels disguised as reality? Or was it deeper—woven into your very being, whispering, "Do more. Be more. Prove you are enough."

But here is the truth they never tell you: You will never silence the voices of the world. The critics. The doubters. The endless comparisons. But you can choose to quiet them within yourself.

Because in the end, all you can do—all you ever needed to do—is your best.

And your best? It will never be perfect. Some days, your best will feel unstoppable—brilliant, expansive, like you have conquered the world. Other days, your best will feel like barely holding yourself together. A whisper. A breath. A small step in the face of overwhelming exhaustion.

But both count. Equally.

Because doing your best is not measured in flawless execution. It is measured in showing up, in giving what you can, in finding a way to rise even when the weight feels unbearable.

Look back at your life. Think of the moments when you felt most defeated—when failure clung to you like a second skin. Did you not rise? Did you not carry on, even when every fibre of your being screamed to stop? You did. And that was enough.

Doing your best never guarantees success. That is the lie they sell you. The truth? Sometimes your best will fall short. Sometimes you will give your all and still face rejection, heartbreak, and loss. And yet—you will rise again.

Because your worth has never been tied to results.

The world glorifies outcomes. Trophies, certificates, applause, success stories wrapped in shiny bows. But the quiet victories? The ones no one sees? Those are where your true strength lies.

The moments you chose kindness when anger felt easier. The times you spoke up when your voice trembled. The nights you stayed awake, wrestling with your doubts, and still woke up determined to give it another shot again.

That is what doing your best means.

It is not about being the strongest, the smartest, or the most successful. It is about integrity—facing the world with honesty, even when it hurts. It is about choosing courage when fear feels overwhelming. It is about compassion—towards yourself and others—when judgment would be easier.

And yes, there will be days when you fall short. When you hurt people. When you let yourself down. But even then, you can still rise. To learn. To offer yourself the same compassion you so freely give to others.

Because the truth is, you are not here to be perfect. You are here to be whole. To live. To stumble. To grow. To love. To forgive. To keep showing up.

EXPLORATION TIME:
What does "doing your best" look like for you, not in the abstract, but in your everyday life?

At the end of the day, ask yourself: Did I show up? Did I give what I could today? Celebrate those moments rather than criticising yourself for what was left undone.

Pause for presence. Am I present with what I am doing right now? Redirect your focus to the task at hand rather than the outcome.

Keep a small notebook where you jot down one thing you did well each day, no matter how small. Over time, this becomes a tangible reminder of your efforts.

Choose one task or goal where you will intentionally let go of the need to do it perfectly. Reflect on how it feels to complete it without perfectionism weighing you down.

When you feel like you have fallen short, practise speaking to yourself as you would a dear friend. What words of compassion would you offer them?

Doing your best is not about achieving perfection. It is about choosing to show up, day after day, even when the world feels overwhelming. It is about understanding that your worth was never tied to trophies or applause, but to the quiet strength that carries you forward when no one is watching.

You will not always get it right. You will stumble. You will fail. And still, your effort, your care, and your resilience will always count. Because in the end, your best is not a result—it is a choice. A practice. A way of being.

To do your best. To be present. To give what you can. And to know—deeply, undeniably—that your best was always, always enough.

REFLECTION QUESTIONS
What does "doing your best" mean to you in this season of life?
How often do you tie your self-worth to results rather than effort?
What would shift if you allowed yourself to feel enough, even on your most challenging days?

The Grace & Beauty of Chaos—And Why It Was Never Chaos After All

"To do the best I can, despite the odds, is my creed. And my best in your eyes may be no good. This is not the path of a victim. It's the journey of a peaceful warrior. This warrior does not battle the world but finds equanimity with the darkness and shadows within. They wield quiet strength, rooted in authenticity and resilience." — Rohit Bassi

"To do the best I can, despite the odds, is my creed." These words transcend the shallow noise of victimhood and echo something far deeper—the unwavering path of a peaceful warrior. One who seeks no fight yet refuses to be conquered. Not by the world. Not by their own darkness.

The peaceful warrior meets chaos not with resistance but with presence. They understand that the storms of life never need taming. Chaos was never the enemy; it was always the teacher—misunderstood because we were too busy trying and hustling to control what was never ours to control.

Life has never been black and white. And neither is chaos. Chaos is not punishment. It is the raw, untamed dance of existence—birth, decay, growth, collapse, love, loss, clarity, confusion—all swirling together, beautifully unfiltered. Yet we call it chaos only because it refuses to fit the tidy boxes we have built in our minds.

But what if it was never chaos at all? What if it was just life, unmasked?

We mistake emotional intensity for chaos too. The moments when a connection feels overwhelming, when love aches more than it comforts, when the heart feels vulnerable yet open—it feels messy, uncontainable. Yet this vulnerability is not weakness. It is the courage to feel fully, without control, without needing to possess or be possessed.

Longing is not the enemy. It is the echo of the heart reminding us that life's deepest truths are rarely tidy. To give your heart, even when it aches, to stand in emotional storms without running from them—that is not chaos. That is the rawness of being fully alive.

I used to believe pain was proof I was broken and still do when I unwillingly restrict myself. That the cracks in my life were evidence of failure, things to be hidden or fixed. But then I began to see differently. The cracks were not imperfections. They were entry points for light. They were part of becoming.

You see, the world sold us this lie—that peace is found in order, perfection, control. That we must conquer our pain, silence our struggles, master every moment to be worthy. But peace is not the absence of chaos. It is making space for it without being consumed.

The peaceful warrior does not seek to eliminate the storm. They learn to stand in it. To dance with it. To see the grace and beauty in the wildness.

Look closely, and you will see there was never chaos—only life unfolding as it must.

Your life is truly The Neverending Story.

Life has no tidy endings. No perfect resolutions. The story continues, chapter after chapter, sometimes or many times repeating the same scenarios in different ways. The idea of "closure" is an illusion. Life never wraps up in neat conclusions—it evolves, it shifts, it leaves loose threads, unanswered questions, unfinished sentences.

But that is where the beauty lies.

You have felt it too, have you not? The messiness of healing. The contradiction of grief and gratitude existing together. The ache of growth paired with the joy of rediscovery. These are not opposites—they belong together, intertwined in the fabric of who you are becoming.

And yes, the patterns repeat—the relationships, the fears, the wounds. But not because you are broken. Because life invites you to learn. To see with new eyes. To break free never by force but by understanding.

You were never meant to win every battle. You were meant to rise from them. Stronger. Softer. Wiser.

You Were Never Broken. You Were Always Becoming.

The peaceful warrior never measures themselves by victories or defeats. They measure by how fully they showed up. By how deeply they felt. By the quiet strength it takes to keep breathing when the world feels unbearable.

So here you are. Not broken. Not defeated. Becoming. And if the storms still rage? If the chaos still feels too loud, too consuming—remember this:

You never needed to fix the storm.
You only needed to trust that you could stand in it.

That was never chaos. That was always grace, waiting for you to see it.

MY CREED: TO DO THE BEST I CAN, DESPITE THE ODDS.

TOOLS OF EXPLORATION FOR RELEASE, CLEANING, HEALING AND TRANSMUTING

These tools are ones I have personally used throughout my life journey and have seen others benefit from as well.

They are designed to foster growth, resilience, and deeper connections, offering practical ways to navigate challenges and find clarity.

These tools, woven through the chapters, offer a robust framework for personal growth, emotional resilience, and meaningful connections.

The tools provided throughout this book are designed to be flexible, adaptable, and deeply personal. Whether you are facing challenges, pain, suffering, or simply navigating the complex themes of life, these tools serve as building blocks for your growth and resilience.

They are not confined to specific chapters but can be revisited and reimagined in different contexts, depending on where you are in your journey.

Use them to reflect, heal, and take actionable steps toward a life aligned with your unique path.

Let these tools be your companions as you embrace life's uncertainties with courage, clarity, conviction, and compassion.

Acknowledging Pain: Recognise and name the emotions or situations that cause discomfort without judgment.

Setting Shields: Establish margins to protect and safeguard emotional and mental well-being.

Seeking Support: Rely on trusted individuals or communities for encouragement and perspective.

Turning Discomfort into Exploration: Use challenging moments as opportunities for self-discovery and growth.

Equanimity Practice: Cultivate inner calm to remain steady in uncertain situations.

Breathe Through Discomfort: Use conscious breathing to anchor yourself in moments of fear or anxiety.

Reframe Beliefs: Challenge and reshape beliefs that limit growth or self-worth.

Reflective Journaling: Explore emotions, beliefs, and experiences through writing to gain clarity.

Symbolic Release: Engage in physical acts like burning letters or symbolic rituals to signify letting go.

Self-Compassion Exercises: Practice treating yourself with kindness and forgiveness.

Facing the Subconscious: Explore hidden patterns through self-inquiry or therapy.

Mantra Meditation: Use specific mantras to calm the mind and shift focus.

Mind-Flow Practice: Embrace fluidity in thoughts and actions, letting go of rigid mindsets.

Radical Acceptance: Embrace situations and emotions without resistance.

Clarify Intentions: Reflect on the motivations behind actions to ensure alignment with values.

Daily Check-ins: Assess emotions, intentions, and accomplishments at the end of each day.

Reflecting on Past Experiences: Look back at challenges and what they taught you.

Listening Fully: Cultivate deep listening to understand others without rushing to respond.

Open-Ended Questions: Use questions like, "What else would you like to share?" to foster deeper dialogue.

Face-it, Faith-it, Make-it Framework: Confront challenges, trust the process, and act with integrity.

Observe Emotional Triggers: Pause and examine reactions to identify underlying beliefs.

Tracking Progress: Celebrate small victories and shifts in perspective.

Pausing Before Action: Create stillness to allow clarity before making decisions.

Visualization Exercises: Imagine desired outcomes or feelings to guide actions.

Ask Better Questions: Replace "Why is this happening?" with "What is this teaching me?"

Gratitude Reflection: Identify and appreciate aspects of life that bring value and joy.

Writing a Raw Letter: Express unfiltered emotions in writing to release pent-up feelings.

Practicing Generosity: Give time, resources, or kindness without expecting anything in return.

Mindfulness Techniques: Stay present through breathwork or grounding exercises.

Strengthening Relationships: Engage in meaningful conversations with those who uplift you.

Feedforward Thinking: Focus on future possibilities and actionable steps rather than dwelling on past mistakes.

Challenge Negative Narratives: Reassess beliefs or stories that perpetuate self-doubt.

Creating Visual Mind Maps: Use diagrams to explore support networks or personal growth paths.

Celebrating Resilience: Recognise and honour personal strength and perseverance.

Engaging in Rituals: Perform simple acts to mark new beginnings or emotional releases.

Learning From Setbacks: View failures as opportunities for growth and understanding.

Flow States: Seek immersive activities that align with your strengths and interests.

Cleansing Practices: Use methods like Ho'oponopono or other spiritual techniques to release emotional burdens.

Simplifying Goals: Break objectives into manageable, intentional steps.

Self-Awareness Exercises: Notice thought patterns, triggers, and behaviours in real-time.

Building Shields: Strengthen emotional defences while staying open to meaningful connections.

Seek Professional Guidance: Turn to therapists, coaches, or mentors when needed.

Redefining Success: Reflect on what success means beyond societal expectations.

Engaging in Self-Inquiry: Use prompts like, "Whose voice is influencing this belief?" to gain clarity.

Grounding in Nature: Spend time in natural settings to restore balance and perspective.

Exploring Philosophical Traditions: Draw wisdom from practices like Buddhism, Stoicism, or Taoism.

Balancing Action with Rest: Recognise when to push forward and when to pause for renewal.

Embracing Solitude: Spend time alone to deepen self-understanding and emotional resilience.

Practicing Gratitude for Challenges: Reflect on how difficulties have shaped personal growth.

Developing Emotional Flexibility: Adapt to life's changes without losing inner stability.

Ho'oponopono: A Hawaiian practice of forgiveness and emotional cleansing.

Nirvana Shatakam: A mantra for grounding and achieving peace.

Thich Nhat Hanh's Teachings: Techniques on mindful breathing and radical acceptance.

Mantra-Based Meditation: Using specific sounds or phrases to centre the mind.

Reiki and Pranic Healing: Energy-based methods to clear emotional or physical blockages.

Cognitive Behavioural Techniques (CBT): Practical approaches for reframing negative thought patterns.

Radical Acceptance Practices: Acknowledging reality fully to reduce suffering.

Vipassana Meditation: Observing sensations and thoughts to cultivate equanimity.

Journaling: A reflective tool for emotional clarity and problem-solving.

Grounding Techniques: Using sensory experiences to anchor in the present moment.

Langar and Seva (Sikhism): Acts of selfless service as tools for connection and humility.

Wu Wei (Taoism): The principle of effortless action by aligning with life's natural flow.

Amor Fati (Stoicism): Loving fate and embracing life's challenges as opportunities.

Symbolic Acts of Release: Rituals for emotional or spiritual closure.

Reflective Dialogue: Engaging in meaningful conversations to deepen understanding and connection.

REFERENCE BOOKS

This book list is a gateway to timeless wisdom, blending ancient philosophies, modern science, and transformative narratives. From spiritual growth to practical insights, each title offers guidance for self-discovery, resilience, and connection. Let these books inspire your journey towards meaning, healing, and purpose.

The Bhagavad Gita – Duty, purpose, and detachment.

Swami Vivekananda – Wisdom from Vedanta and spiritual growth.

Guru Granth Sahib – Spiritual teachings from Sikhism.

Autobiography of a Yogi by Paramahansa Yogananda – Mysticism and self-realisation.

The Complete Works of Swami Vivekananda – Insights into Vedanta and self-realisation.

I Am That by Nisargadatta Maharaj – Profound self-inquiry and liberation.

Jiddu Krishnamurti – Teachings on inner freedom and truth.

The Upanishads – Exploring the nature of self and ultimate reality.

Awakening the A C E by Dr. Segu Krishna Ramesh – Realisation of abundance and consciousness.

The Essential Rumi – Soulful poetry on love and spirituality.

The Rubaiyat of Omar Khayyam – Joy and impermanence.

The Prophet by Kahlil Gibran – Universal truths in lyrical prose.

Long Walk to Freedom by Nelson Mandela – Resilience and leadership.

Things Fall Apart by Chinua Achebe – Change and identity.

Ubuntu: I Am Because We Are by Mungi Ngomane – Interconnection and compassion.

Man's Search for Meaning by Viktor E. Frankl – Purpose in suffering.

Power vs. Force by Sir David R. Hawkins – Levels of consciousness.

Feel the Fear and Do It Anyway® by Susan Jeffers – Overcoming fear with courage.

The Biology of Belief by Bruce H. Lipton – Consciousness and healing.

A Course in Miracles (ACIM) by Helen Schucman – A spiritual guide to miracles.

A Return to Love by Marianne Williamson –
Reflections on ACIM.

Jonathan Livingston Seagull by Richard Bach –
Breaking barriers and self-discovery.

The Art of Happiness by the Dalai Lama and
Howard Cutler – Inner peace and joy.

Happiness Now! by Robert Holden – Timeless
wisdom for feeling good.

The Compassionate Instinct edited by Dacher
Keltner, Jason Marsh, and Jeremy Adam Smith –
Exploring human goodness.

Braiding Sweetgrass by Robin Wall Kimmerer –
Interconnection with nature.

The Sacred Pipe by Black Elk – Lakota spiritual
teachings.

Wisdom Sits in Places by Keith H. Basso – Native
American storytelling.

The Book of Five Rings by Miyamoto Musashi –
Samurai discipline and strategy.

Bushido: The Soul of Japan by Inazo Nitobe –
Samurai code of honour.

Ikigai-Kan: Feel a Life Worth Living by Nicholas
Kemp – Authentic Japanese philosophy of purpose.

Atomic Habits by James Clear – Building lasting
habits.

Daring Greatly by Brené Brown – Courage and vulnerability.

The Gifts of Imperfection by Brené Brown – Wholehearted living.

Essentialism by Greg McKeown – Clarity and focus.

Flow by Mihaly Csikszentmihalyi – Engagement and fulfilment.

The User Illusion by Tor Norretranders – Exploring the limits of consciousness.

The Wisdom of Insecurity by Alan Watts – Embracing uncertainty.

Mindfulness in Plain English by Bhante Henepola Gunaratana – Practical mindfulness.

Letting Go by David R. Hawkins – Emotional release and surrender.

Who's in Charge? by Dr. Ihaleakala Hew Len – Exploring **Ho'oponopono**, taking responsibility for healing.

When the Body Says No by Dr. Gabor Maté – Understanding the mind-body connection in illness.

The Myth of Normal by Dr. Gabor Maté – Trauma, health, and healing in modern society.

In the Realm of Hungry Ghosts by Dr. Gabor Maté – Addiction, trauma, and compassion in healing.

Gitanjali by Rabindranath Tagore – Poetic meditations on life and spirituality.

Sea and Sardinia by D.H. Lawrence – Reflective travel writing.

The Leader Who Had No Title by Robin Sharma – Leadership and purpose.

Lead from the Outside by Stacey Abrams – Overcoming challenges.

Start with Why by Simon Sinek – Inspiring action through purpose.

The Long Road Turns to Joy by Thich Nhat Hanh – Walking through challenges.

Humankind: A Hopeful History by Rutger Bregman – The innate goodness of humanity.

Living Buddha, Living Christ by Thich Nhat Hanh – Interfaith harmony.

The Heart of the Buddha's Teaching by Thich Nhat Hanh – Four Noble Truths and mindfulness.

A New Earth by Eckhart Tolle – Presence and ego dissolution.

RESEARCH PAPERS

This collection of research papers bridges rigorous inquiry with profound insight, offering a foundation for understanding life's complexities.

Each paper explores themes of resilience, growth, relationships, and human potential through the lens of evidence-based knowledge.

Let these works guide and inspire your journey toward deeper awareness, healing, and purposeful living.

The Philosophical Significance of the Bhagavad Gita
– Sharma, A. (1986). Philosophy East and West. Explores ethical and spiritual teachings.

Vedanta Philosophy and the Modern Interpretation of Swami Vivekananda
– Flood, G. (1996). Oxford University Press.

The Role of the Guru Granth Sahib in Sikhism
– Mandair, A.-P. (2013). Journal of Religious Studies.

Logotherapy and Existential Analysis: Theoretical Foundations
– Frankl, V. (1985). International Forum for Logotherapy.

Energy Fields in Consciousness Research
– Hawkins, D. R. (2002). Consciousness Studies Review.

Epigenetics and the Mind-Body Connection
– Lipton, B. H. (2004). Journal of Molecular Biology.
Fear, Coping, and Behavioural Change: A

Psychological Perspective
– Lazarus, R. S., & Folkman, S. (1984). Psychological Inquiry.

The Role of Trauma in Addiction and Healing
– Maté, G. (2004). Psychology Today.

Stress and Chronic Illness: A Mind-Body Perspective
– Maté, G. (2003). Journal of Health Psychology.
Ho'oponopono as a Therapeutic Practice
– Hew Len, I. (2007). Journal of Transpersonal Psychology.

Restoration Ecology and Indigenous Knowledge Systems
– Kimmerer, R. W. (2012). Frontiers in Ecology and the Environment.

Place-Making and Cultural Significance
– Basso, K. H. (1996). Cultural Anthropology.

Self-Determination Theory and Its Impact on Leadership
– Ryan, R. M., & Deci, E. L. (2000). Psychological Inquiry.

Habit Formation and Behavioural Change
– Wood, W., & Neal, D. T. (2007). Annual Review of Psychology.

The Concept of Ikigai in Japanese Culture
– Mathews, G. (1996). Ethos Journal.

Philosophical Applications of Bushido and Strategy
– Wilson, W. (2004). Asian Studies Journal.

Meditation, Emotional Regulation, and Neuroplasticity
– Davidson, R. J., & Kabat-Zinn, J. (2003). Journal of Clinical Psychology.

The Science of Compassion and Its Evolutionary Significance
– Keltner, D., & Goetz, J. L. (2007). Science and Emotion.